# The Heart Healthy Cookbook for Beginners:

Easy Flavorful Recipes to Lower Cholesterol and Blood Pressure, Embrace Clean Eating and Start Your Journey to Lifelong Wellness

Alexandra Morgan

# TABLE OF CONTENTS

# INTRODUCTION

## Welcome to Heart-Healthy American Cooking

Greetings, fellow food enthusiasts and health-conscious cooks! I'm thrilled to embark on this journey with you through the pages of the "Heart Healthy Cookbook for Beginners." This volume is more than a collection of recipes; it's a guide to transforming your relationship with food into one that favors your heart's well-being. Here, you'll find a trove of dishes that tantalize the palate while nurturing the most vital organ in your body.

My mission is to show that heart-healthy eating doesn't mean sacrificing flavor or enjoyment. With every recipe, we'll explore delicious ways to incorporate nutrient-rich ingredients into your diet, ensuring each meal brings joy and health to your table. Whether you're an experienced chef or a newcomer to the culinary world, this book is crafted to inspire and aid you in creating dishes that are both mouthwatering and beneficial for your heart.

## Making the Shift: Easy Steps to a Healthier Heart

Eating with your heart in mind doesn't require a drastic overhaul of your diet overnight. It's about making small, manageable changes that add up to significant health benefits. In this section, we'll discuss straightforward swaps and gradual alterations that ease the transition to a heart-healthy lifestyle. Each recipe you'll discover within these pages promotes a positive step forward in this journey, providing a foundation for lasting well-being.

## Deciphering Heart Health: A Nutritional Overview

Understanding the connection between the foods you eat and your heart health is powerful. This cookbook takes you through the maze of nutritional science and offers clarity on why certain foods are particularly beneficial for your cardiovascular health. We'll go over the key elements that support a heart-friendly diet, emphasizing whole, unprocessed foods; in particular, we'll focus on those that lower blood pressure, bad cholesterol, and heart disease risk.

## Essential Kitchen Tools for the Heart-Healthy Cook

A well-equipped kitchen is your best ally for creating heart-healthy meals. It doesn't require a professional setup—you'll be surprised at how few tools you need to prepare the majority of these recipes. We'll outline the kitchen essentials that streamline the cooking process and discuss how some gadgets can help you reduce unhealthy fats, salts, and sugars without diminishing the taste and pleasure of eating.

As you turn the pages, let your appetite for good, wholesome food be your guide. Cook, taste, and savor with the knowledge that each recipe leads you to a healthier heart. So tie on your apron, heat up that skillet, and ready your taste buds for a delightful culinary adventure that's as good for your heart as it is for your soul. Welcome to heart-healthy cooking!

Now, let's get started and dive into the delicious and nourishing world of the "Heart Healthy Cookbook for Beginners."

## How to Stay Motivated on a Heart-Healthy Diet

Staying motivated on a heart-healthy diet can sometimes be a challenge, especially with the abundance of tempting, less nutritious options at every turn. However, by employing the following strategies, you can maintain your resolve and consistently make choices that benefit your heart:

1. Set Realistic Goals: Start with achievable objectives, like incorporating a vegetable into each meal or cooking at home three times a week. Reach these small goals before tackling more ambitious changes.
2. Educate Yourself: Understanding the "why" behind heart-healthy eating can be a powerful motivator. Educational Insights, like those provided in our cookbook, shed light on the impact of diet on heart health and long-term well-being.
3. Plan and Prep Your Meals: A Visual Delight in meal planning can help you stick to your diet. Prep components of your meals in advance, like chopping veggies or making sauces, to alleviate the stress of cooking from scratch each day.
4. Keep It Interesting: Continuously explore new recipes and flavors to prevent dietary boredom. A diverse range of heart-healthy recipes, including international dishes adapted for global audiences, can help keep your menu exciting.
5. Indulge Occasionally: Allowing yourself an occasional treat can make a restrictive diet feel more manageable. Pick heart-healthy indulgences that satisfy your cravings without derailing your diet.
6. Track Your Progress: Journaling your meals and how you feel can help you see the positive impact of your diet on your health and motivate you to continue.
7. Enlist Support: Surround yourself with a support system, whether it's family, friends, or online communities, that can encourage your journey and keep you accountable.
8. Reward Success: Celebrate your milestones in heart-healthy eating. Whether it's sticking to your diet for a full week or noticing improvements in your health, acknowledging these achievements can boost your drive to persist.
9. Focus on the Benefits: Keep in mind the benefits of a heart-healthy diet, such as increased energy, improved health markers, and a reduced risk of chronic diseases.
10. Be Flexible: If you stray from your diet, don't be too hard on yourself. Acknowledge the slip-up and get back on track with your next meal.

Remember, a heart-healthy diet is a lifelong journey, and each heart-conscious choice contributes to a stronger, healthier heart. Stay motivated by reflecting on your progress, the delicious foods you can enjoy, and the long-term health benefits you're working toward.

## Shopping List and Pantry Staples

Creating a shopping list of pantry staples is an excellent way to ensure you always have the key ingredients on hand for preparing heart-healthy meals. Here's a comprehensive list that covers the essentials:

Pantry Staples:

Whole Grains:
- Brown rice
- Quinoa
- Whole-grain pasta
- Rolled oats
- Barley
- Bulgur
- Whole-grain bread and tortillas

Legumes:
- Lentils
- Chickpeas
- Black beans
- Kidney beans
- Navy beans

Nuts and Seeds:
- Almonds
- Walnuts
- Chia seeds
- Flaxseeds
- Pumpkin seeds
- Sunflower seeds

**Healthy Oils:**
- Extra virgin olive oil
- Avocado oil
- Coconut oil (unrefined)

**Vinegars:**
- Apple cider vinegar
- Balsamic vinegar
- Red wine vinegar
- White wine vinegar

**Canned Goods:**
- Low-sodium vegetable broth
- Canned low-sodium beans
- Canned tomatoes (no added salt)
- Light coconut milk

**Herbs and Spices:**
- Fresh or dried basil
- Thyme
- Oregano
- Parsley
- Cilantro
- Rosemary
- Ground cinnamon
- Ground turmeric
- Cayenne pepper
- Garlic powder
- Onion powder
- Black pepper
- Sea salt or Himalayan pink salt

**Condiments:**
- Mustard (look for low sodium options)
- Salsa (no added sugar)
- Low-sodium soy sauce or tamari
- Nutritional yeast

**Sweeteners:**
- Honey
- Maple syrup

**Other:**
- Unsweetened applesauce

**Refrigerator Staples:**

**Dairy or Dairy Alternatives:**
- Low-fat or nonfat Greek yogurt
- Low-fat or nonfat milk or plant-based milk (almond, soy, oat)
- Low-fat cheese varieties

**Proteins:**
- Fresh or frozen lean meats like chicken or turkey breast
- Fresh or frozen fish like salmon, mackerel, or trout
- Eggs or egg substitutes
- Tofu
- Tempeh

**Fruits and Vegetables:**
- A variety of fresh fruits (apples, berries, pears, oranges)
- A variety of fresh vegetables (leafy greens, bell peppers, carrots, broccoli)
- Garlic
- Onions

**Freezer Staples:**

**Vegetables:**
- Frozen mixed vegetables (without added sauces or seasonings)
- Frozen spinach or kale
- Frozen peas and carrots

**Fruits:**
- Frozen berries
- Frozen mango
- Frozen bananas (for smoothies)

**Proteins:**
- Frozen lean meats
- Frozen seafood

Having these items stocked will allow you to create nutritious meals that benefit heart health, ensuring fiber, protein, healthy fats, and a multitude of vitamins and minerals are a part of your daily diet. Remember to adjust the list according to your dietary preferences and restrictions.

# Cooking Techniques to Maximize Nutrient Retention

Maximizing nutrient retention during cooking is key to a heart-healthy diet. Some nutrients can be lost during the cooking process, so it's beneficial to use methods that preserve the nutritive content of your food. Here are several techniques to help retain the maximum amount of nutrients:

1. Steaming: This gentle cooking method preserves the integrity of vitamins and minerals, especially in vegetables. Using a steamer basket helps to retain most of the food's nutrients since it prevents the vegetables from soaking in water, which can leach out water-soluble vitamins like vitamins C and B vitamins.
2. Roasting and Baking: Cooking foods at a lower temperature in the oven can preserve nutrients better than high-temperature methods. Roasting and baking can also enhance flavors without adding extra fats or oils.
3. Grilling: Grilling can be a heart-healthy method when done correctly. It requires minimal added fat and can create intense flavor. However, it's important to prevent charring, as burnt portions can contain harmful compounds. Use marinades to help protect the food's surface and add antioxidants.
4. Sautéing: Quick cooking at medium to high heat in a small amount of healthy oil, like olive or avocado oil, is an excellent way to cook while preserving the taste and nutrients. This method works well for a variety of foods, from vegetables to lean meats and fish.
5. Blanching: Submerging foods briefly in boiling water and then placing them into ice water can help retain color, flavor, and nutrients. This method is especially good for green vegetables like broccoli or spinach.
6. Poaching: Cooking at a lower temperature in a simmering liquid that just barely bubbles can yield tender meat and vegetables full of nutrients. It's a particularly good technique for delicate foods such as eggs, fish, and fruit.
7. Pressure Cooking: Using a pressure cooker can drastically reduce cooking times and thus can help preserve nutrients that might otherwise be lost to prolonged heat exposure.
8. Microwaving: This can be a nutrient-saving cooking method as it shortens cooking times and uses minimal liquid. However, be mindful not to overcook as this will diminish the nutrient density.
9. Raw Preparations: Incorporating raw foods into your diet, like salads or crudités, ensures that you consume all the natural nutrients without any loss from cooking.
10. Minimal Water Usage: When boiling is necessary, use as little water as possible to reduce nutrient loss, and consider using the cooking water in your dish to take advantage of the nutrients that leached into it.

Remember to always cook with fresh, high-quality ingredients, and avoid overcooking your meals to ensure you are getting the most nutrients out of your heart-healthy diet.

## Nutritional Information (per serving):
Please note that the amounts and brands of certain products used may cause variations in the nutritional values shown. Use a nutrition calculator using the selected ingredients for precise information.

# CHAPTER 1: MORNING STARTS

## 1.1 Berry Bliss Oatmeal

**Servings: 2 | Preparation Time: 5 minutes | Cooking Time: 10 minutes**

### INGREDIENTS:

* 1 cup (80g) rolled oats
* 2 cups (480ml) water or milk (for a creamier texture)
* Pinch of salt
* 1/2 teaspoon ground cinnamon
* 1 tablespoon honey or pure maple syrup (optional)
* 1/2 cup (75g) fresh mixed berries (such as strawberries, blueberries, raspberries)
* 2 tablespoons chopped almonds or walnuts
* 1 tablespoon chia seeds (optional)
* 1/4 cup (60g) Greek yogurt for topping (optional)

### INSTRUCTIONS:

1. Heat the milk or water in a medium pot until it boils. Add a pinch of salt and rolled oats. Lower the temperature to medium-low and let it cook for five minutes, stirring now and again.
2. Stir in the ground cinnamon and continue to cook until the oats are soft and have absorbed most of the liquid, about another 5 minutes.
3. Remove the oatmeal from the stove and let it sit for 2 minutes to thicken even more.
4. If preferred, sweeten the oatmeal with honey or maple syrup before dividing it into two bowls.
5. For extra texture and nutrients, top each bowl of oats with a generous handful of mixed berries and add chopped almonds and chia seeds.
6. If you like, dollop Greek yogurt on top of each serving for creaminess and an extra protein boost.
7. Serve immediately while warm, and enjoy the burst of berry flavors with each spoonful!

### Nutritional Information (per serving):

• Calories: 300 kcal • Protein: 11g • Carbohydrates: 45g • Fat: 9g (1.5g saturated fat) • Cholesterol: 5mg
• Sodium: 75mg • Dietary Fiber: 8g • Sugars: 10g

---

## 1.2 Avocado and Heirloom Tomato Toast

**Servings: 2 | Preparation Time: 10 minutes | Cooking Time: 5 minutes**

### INGREDIENTS:

* 4 slices of whole-grain bread
* 1 large ripe avocado
* 1 small heirloom tomato, sliced
* Salt and pepper to taste
* 1 tablespoon olive oil
* Fresh basil leaves for garnish
* Optional: red pepper flakes and a drizzle of balsamic glaze

### INSTRUCTIONS:

1. Start by toasting the whole-grain bread to your preferred level of crispness. Toast each slice for about 2 minutes on each side using a toaster or a non-stick pan heated to medium heat.

2. Cut the avocado in half, remove the pit, and scoop out the flesh into a bowl while the bread is browning.

3. Mash the avocado with a fork until it reaches a smooth consistency, using some small chunks for texture. Season with salt and pepper to taste.

4. Once the bread is toasted, brush each slice lightly with olive oil for a rich flavor and heart-healthy fats.

5. Spread the mashed avocado evenly across the toasted bread slices.

6. Layer the heirloom tomato slices on top of the avocado. If you enjoy a little spice, feel free to add a pinch of red pepper flakes.

7. For a pleasant touch, tear fresh basil leaves and sprinkle them over the toast.

8. If desired, drizzle a small amount of balsamic glaze over the toasts for a sweet and tangy finish.

9. Serve immediately and enjoy the fresh, vibrant flavors!

**Nutritional Information (per serving):**

• Calories: 320 kcal • Protein: 9g • Carbohydrates: 38g • Fat: 16g • Saturated Fat: 2.5g • Cholesterol: 0mg
• Sodium: 300mg • Dietary Fiber: 9g • Sugars: 5g

## 1.3 Greek Yogurt with Honeyed Walnuts and Figs

**Servings: 2 | Preparation Time: 5 minutes | Cooking Time: 0 minutes**

**INGREDIENTS:**

• 2 cups (480g) Greek yogurt (unsweetened)
• 1/4 cup (30g) walnuts, chopped
• 4 fresh figs, quartered
• 2 tablespoons (30ml) honey
• Optional: A pinch of ground cinnamon or cardamom

**INSTRUCTIONS:**

1. Divide the Greek yogurt equally between two serving bowls.

2. Toast the chopped walnuts gently in a small pan over medium heat until fragrant and brown.

3. Be careful, as nuts can burn quickly, so keep an eye on them and stir often. This should take about 2-3 minutes.

4. Once toasted, allow the nuts to cool slightly. If you'd like, you can then toss them with a pinch of ground cinnamon or cardamom for added flavor.

5. Place the quartered fresh figs on top of the Greek yogurt, distributing them evenly between the two servings.

6. Drizzle the honey over each serving of yogurt and figs, allowing it to sink in and sweeten the dish.

7. Sprinkle the toasted (and optionally spiced) walnuts over the top, adding a delightful crunch.

8. Serve immediately, enjoying the combination of creamy yogurt, sweet honey, and figs, and the warm spice and crunch of toasted walnuts.

**Nutritional Information (per serving):**

• Calories: 290 kcal • Protein: 20g • Carbohydrates: 37g • Fat: 9g • Saturated Fat: 1g • Cholesterol: 10mg
• Sodium: 65mg • Dietary Fiber: 3g • Sugars: 28g (includes natural sugars from honey and figs)

## 1.4 Chia Seed and Kiwi Parfait

Servings: 2 | Preparation Time: 15 minutes | Chilling Time: At least 4 hours or overnight

**INGREDIENTS:**

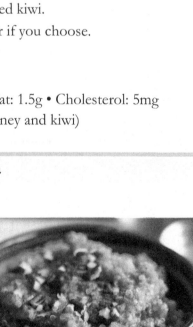

- 1/4 cup (60g) chia seeds
- 1 cup (240ml) unsweetened almond milk or any milk of your choice
- 2 kiwis, peeled and diced
- 1/2 cup (120g) Greek yogurt, unsweetened
- 1 tablespoon honey or maple syrup (optional for added sweetness)
- Optional toppings: Sliced almonds, coconut flakes, or additional fruit

**INSTRUCTIONS:**

1. In a mixing bowl, combine chia seeds with almond milk and stir thoroughly. For a hint of sweetness, feel free to add honey or maple syrup.
2. Cover the bowl and refrigerate for at least 4 hours or, ideally, overnight. A pudding-like substance will be produced when the chia seeds expand and absorb the liquid.
3. The chia seed mixture should be thoroughly stirred while serving. To achieve the correct consistency, thin it out a bit by adding a little extra milk.
4. Spoon half of the chia seed mixture into two serving glasses, creating the first layer of your parfait.
5. Place a layer of Greek yogurt in each glass on top of the chia mixture.
6. Arrange half of the diced kiwi on top of the yogurt layer.
7. Repeat the layering with the remaining chia mixture, Greek yogurt, and diced kiwi.
8. Garnish with sliced almonds or coconut flakes for added texture and flavor if you choose.
9. Serve and enjoy this nutrient-packed, vibrant parfait!

**Nutritional Information (per serving):**

• Calories: 280 kcal • Protein: 11g • Carbohydrates: 30g • Fat: 14g • Saturated Fat: 1.5g • Cholesterol: 5mg
• Sodium: 120mg • Dietary Fiber: 15g • Sugars: 10g (natural sugars from the honey and kiwi)

## 1.5 Pumpkin Spice Breakfast Quinoa

Servings: 2 | Preparation Time: 5 minutes | Cooking Time: 20 minutes

**INGREDIENTS:**

- 1/2 cup (90g) quinoa, rinsed and drained
- 1 cup (240ml) unsweetened almond milk, plus more for serving
- 1/2 cup (120g) pumpkin puree (not pumpkin pie filling)
- 1/2 teaspoon ground cinnamon
- 1/4 teaspoon ground nutmeg
- 1/4 teaspoon ground ginger
- A pinch of ground cloves
- 1-2 tablespoons (15-30ml) maple syrup, to taste
- Optional toppings: Chopped nuts, a dollop of Greek yogurt, fresh fruit, or an additional sprinkle of cinnamon

**INSTRUCTIONS:**

1. Combine the rinsed quinoa and almond milk in a medium saucepan. Heat the mixture on medium-high and bring it to a boil.

2. After the quinoa is soft and most of the milk has been absorbed, lower the heat to a simmer for 15 minutes while covered.

3. Stir in the pumpkin puree, cinnamon, nutmeg, ginger, and cloves, mixing until well combined.

4. Stirring occasionally, simmer the mixture for an additional 5 minutes. To get the appropriate consistency, adjust the mixture's thickness by adding extra almond milk if necessary.

5. Taste the quinoa and add maple syrup according to your sweetness preference. Stir well.

6. Divide the pumpkin spice quinoa into two serving bowls.

7. Add your choice of toppings, such as chopped nuts for additional heart-healthy fats and proteins, Greek yogurt for a creamy tang, or fresh fruit for natural sweetness and fiber.

8. Serve warm with an extra dash of almond milk or another drizzle of maple syrup if desired.

## Nutritional Information (per serving):

• Calories: 315 kcal • Protein: 8g • Carbohydrates: 55g • Fat: 7g • Saturated Fat: 0.5g • Cholesterol: 0mg
• Sodium: 95mg • Dietary Fiber: 6g • Sugars: 12g

---

# 1.6 Power Green Smoothie

**Servings: 2 | Preparation Time: 5 minutes | Blending Time: 2 minutes**

## INGREDIENTS:

• 2 cups (60g) fresh spinach leaves, thoroughly washed
• 1 medium ripe banana, previously sliced and frozen
• 1/2 cup (122g) frozen mango chunks
• 1/2 an avocado, pitted and scooped
• 1 tablespoon (15g) chia seeds
• 2 cups (480ml) unsweetened almond milk or water
• Optional: A squeeze of fresh lemon or lime juice for added zest

## INSTRUCTIONS:

1. Start by placing the spinach leaves in the blender, followed by the frozen banana and mango chunks, avocado, and chia seeds.

2. Pour the unsweetened almond milk or water over the ingredients in the blender. If you prefer a thinner smoothie, you may add more liquid.

3. If using, add a squeeze of fresh lemon or lime juice now for a bit of tang and vitamin C.

4. Process the ingredients at a high speed until they become creamy and smooth. If necessary, stop the blender to scrape down the sides and continue to blend until no chunks remain.

5. Once blended to your liking, taste the smoothie and adjust the sweetness or acidity. If it's not sweet enough, you could add a small amount of honey or maple syrup.

6. Serve the Power Green Smoothie immediately, pour it into two glasses, and enjoy the refreshing taste and energy boost.

## Nutritional Information (per serving):

• Calories: 245 kcal • Protein: 5g • Carbohydrates: 30g • Fat: 12g • Saturated Fat: 1.5g • Cholesterol: 0mg
• Sodium: 200mg • Dietary Fiber: 9g • Sugars: 16g

# 1.7 Heart-Healthy Blueberry Pancakes

Servings: 2 | Preparation Time: 10 minutes | Cooking Time: 10 minutes

## INGREDIENTS:

- 1 cup (120g) whole wheat flour
- 1 tablespoon (15g) ground flaxseed
- 1 teaspoon (5g) baking powder
- 1/4 teaspoon (1g) baking soda
- A pinch of salt
- 1 cup (240ml) unsweetened almond milk or any milk of your choice
- 1 large egg
- 1 tablespoon (15ml) honey or pure maple syrup
- 1/2 teaspoon (2.5ml) pure vanilla extract
- 3/4 cup (75g) fresh or frozen blueberries (if frozen, do not thaw)
- Non-stick cooking spray or a small amount of oil for the pan
- Optional: Extra blueberries for serving and a dollop of Greek yogurt

## INSTRUCTIONS:

1. To make a well in the middle, stir together the whole wheat flour, ground flaxseed, baking powder, baking soda, and salt in a big basin.
2. Mix the milk, egg, honey, and vanilla essence thoroughly in a separate basin.
3. After carefully mixing until just incorporated, pour the wet components into the dry ingredient thoroughly. Take care not to overmix; a few lumps are acceptable.
4. Mix the blueberries into the batter gently.
5. A non-stick frying pan should be slightly oiled or coated with cooking spray before being heated to medium heat.
6. For each pancake, pour 1/4 cup (60ml) of batter into the pan and cook for 2 to 3 minutes, or until bubbles start to form on the surface and the edges start to firm.
7. After carefully flipping the pancake, cook it for a further 2 minutes, or until it is cooked through and golden brown.
8. Proceed with the leftover batter, modifying the temperature as necessary to avoid scorching.
9. If preferred, top the pancakes with more blueberries and a dollop of Greek yogurt before serving them warm.

## Nutritional Information (per serving):

- Calories: 295 kcal • Protein: 11g • Carbohydrates: 53g • Fat: 5g • Saturated Fat: 1g • Cholesterol: 93mg
- Sodium: 367mg • Dietary Fiber: 8g • Sugars: 12g

# Chapter 2: Wholesome Snacks

## 2.1 Crunchy Kale Chips

**Servings: 2 | Preparation Time: 10 minutes | Cooking Time: 15 minutes**

**INGREDIENTS:**

- 1 large bunch of kale, stems removed and leaves torn into bite-sized pieces
- 1 tablespoon (15ml) olive oil
- 1/4 teaspoon (1g) sea salt
- Optional seasonings: Paprika, garlic powder, or nutritional yeast for added flavor

**INSTRUCTIONS:**

1. Preheat your oven to 300 degrees F (150 degrees C).
2. To ensure that the kale leaves get crispy, give them a good wash and let them air dry.
3. In a large bowl, toss the dry kale pieces with olive oil and sea salt, ensuring each leaf is lightly but evenly coated. If using, add your choice of optional seasonings at this time and toss again.
4. Place the kale leaves in a single layer on a baking sheet covered with parchment paper. Make sure the leaves are not overlapping, as this will steam them instead of crisping them.
5. Bake the leaves for about 10 minutes in a preheated oven, then turn them over and continue baking for another 5-10 minutes, or until the edges are crisp but not browned.
6. Keep a close eye on them, as they can go from perfect to burnt very quickly.
7. When they are done, take them out of the oven and let them sit for a few minutes on the baking sheet; as they cool, they will get even crispier.

**Nutritional Information (per serving):**

• Calories: 150 kcal • Protein: 5g • Carbohydrates: 18g • Fat: 7g • Saturated Fat: 1g • Cholesterol: 0mg
• Sodium: 300mg • Dietary Fiber: 3g • Sugars: 0g

## 2.2 Almond Butter and Banana Rice Cakes

**Servings: 2 | Preparation Time: 5 minutes**

**INGREDIENTS:**

- 2 plain rice cakes
- 2 tablespoons (30g) almond butter
- 1 medium banana, sliced
- Optional toppings: A sprinkle of cinnamon or chia seeds for added flavor and nutrition

**INSTRUCTIONS:**

1. Take two plain rice cakes as your base for a quick and easy snack.
2. Evenly distribute one tablespoon of almond butter over each rice cake.
3. Top the almond butter with banana slices, covering the surface of each rice cake.
4. To add more flavor and nutrition to the banana slices, feel free to sprinkle on some chia seeds or cinnamon.

**Nutritional Information (per serving):**

• Calories: 195 kcal • Protein: 4g • Carbohydrates: 27g • Fat: 8g • Saturated Fat: 1g • Cholesterol: 0mg
• Sodium: 40mg • Dietary Fiber: 4g • Sugars: 10g

## 2.3 Vegetable Nori Rolls

Servings: 2 (about 4 rolls) | Preparation Time: 20 minutes

**INGREDIENTS:**

- 2 sheets of nori (seaweed paper)
- 1 cup (190g) cooked sushi rice or brown rice, cooled
- 1/2 cucumber, julienned
- 1 carrot, julienned
- 1/2 red bell pepper, julienned
- 1/2 avocado, sliced
- 1 tablespoon (15ml) rice vinegar (optional for sushi rice flavor)
- A splash of low-sodium soy sauce or tamari for dipping
- Optional fillings: cooked spinach, sprouts, or tofu for added variety and protein

**INSTRUCTIONS:**

1. If you're using sushi rice, mix in the rice vinegar for added flavor before cooling the rice. For a healthier option, you can also use brown rice, which doesn't require vinegar.
2. Position a nori sheet onto a parchment paper or bamboo sushi mat.
3. Spread half a cup of rice thinly over the nori, leaving about an inch uncovered at the far edge of the sheet after wetting your hands to avoid sticking.
4. Place julienned vegetables and avocado slices in a line across the center of the rice.
5. Begin rolling the nori tightly from the edge nearest to you, using the mat or parchment to pull it snugly and create a cylindrical shape. Use a bit of water to moisten the exposed edge of the nori and seal the roll.
6. The roll should be divided into six equal pieces using a sharp, moist knife.
7. Repeat the process with the remaining ingredients to make another roll.
8. Serve the vegetable nori rolls with a small dish of low-sodium soy sauce or tamari for dipping.

Nutritional Information (per serving - 2 rolls): • Calories: 260 kcal • Protein: 6g • Carbohydrates: 38g • Fat: 10g • Saturated Fat: 1.5g • Cholesterol: 0mg • Sodium: 200mg • Dietary Fiber: 6g • Sugars: 3g

## 2.4 Apple and Walnut Bites with Cinnamon

Servings: 2 | Preparation Time: 5 minutes

**INGREDIENTS:**

- 2 large apples (such as Honeycrisp or Granny Smith)
- 2 tablespoons (30g) chopped walnuts
- 1 teaspoon ground cinnamon
- A pinch of salt
- Optional: A drizzle of honey or a sprinkle of chia seeds for extra sweetness and nutrition

**INSTRUCTIONS:**

1. Wash and core the apples, then cut them into bite-sized pieces or wedges.
2. Add the ground cinnamon, chopped walnuts, and a little amount of salt to a small bowl.
3. Place the apple bites on a serving plate or in a snack bowl.
4. Sprinkle the walnut and cinnamon mixture over the apple bites.
5. For additional flavor and health benefits, consider drizzling a bit of honey or sprinkling some chia seeds on top.

**Nutritional Information (per serving):**

• Calories: 229 kcal • Protein: 2g • Carbohydrates: 37g • Fat: 10g • Saturated Fat: 1g • Cholesterol: 0mg • Sodium: 39mg • Dietary Fiber: 6g • Sugars: 28g (includes natural sugars from apples)

## 2.5 Carrot and Hummus Pinwheels

**Servings: 2 | Preparation Time: 15 minutes**

**INGREDIENTS:**

- 2 large whole wheat tortillas
- 4 tablespoons (60g) hummus
- 1 large carrot, shredded
- 1 cup (30g) fresh spinach leaves, rinsed and patted dry
- Optional: A sprinkle of paprika or cumin for extra spice

**INSTRUCTIONS:**

1. Place the whole wheat tortillas in a tidy, level layer.
2. Spread two tablespoons of hummus on each tortilla, covering them up to the edges.
3. Evenly distribute the shredded carrot on top of the hummus on both tortillas.
4. Lay half a cup of fresh spinach leaves on each tortilla over the layer of carrots.
5. If desired, add a sprinkle of your chosen spice, such as paprika or cumin, for an additional flavor kick.
6. Carefully roll up the tortillas tightly, ensuring the fillings stay in place.
7. With a sharp knife, slice the rolled tortillas into 1-inch pinwheels.
8. Arrange the pinwheels on a plate and serve as a fun and healthy snack or appetizer.

**Nutritional Information (per serving):**

• Calories: 185 kcal • Protein: 6g • Carbohydrates: 28g • Fat: 7g • Saturated Fat: 1g • Cholesterol: 0mg
• Sodium: 320mg • Dietary Fiber: 6g • Sugars: 4g

## 2.6 Edamame and Sesame Toast

**Servings: 2 | Preparation Time: 10 minutes**

**INGREDIENTS:**

- 4 slices of whole-grain bread
- 1 cup (150g) shelled edamame beans, thawed if frozen
- 1 tablespoon (15g) tahini (sesame seed paste)
- 1 clove garlic, minced
- 2 teaspoons (10ml) lemon juice
- 1 tablespoon (15ml) olive oil
- 1 teaspoon sesame seeds
- Salt and pepper to taste
- Optional: Red pepper flakes or sliced green onions for garnish

**INSTRUCTIONS:**

1. Toast the whole grain bread slices until they are crisp and light golden brown.
2. Process the edamame, tahini, garlic, and lemon juice in a food processor until a spreadable paste forms. If necessary, add a little water or olive oil to adjust the consistency.
3. Season the edamame mixture with salt and pepper to taste.
4. Spread the edamame paste evenly on the toasted whole-grain bread slices.
5. Over each piece, drizzle a little olive oil.
6. Sprinkle sesame seeds on top, adding a nutty crunch to your toast.
7. If you like, garnish with red pepper flakes or sliced green onions for an extra kick and a pop of color.

**Nutritional Information (per serving - 2 slices):**

• Calories: 320 kcal • Protein: 16g • Carbohydrates: 31g • Fat: 16g • Saturated Fat: 2g • Cholesterol: 0mg
• Sodium: 200mg • Dietary Fiber: 9g • Sugars: 3g

## 2.7 Spiced Pumpkin Seeds

**Servings: 2 | Preparation Time: 30 minutes**

**INGREDIENTS:**

- 1 cup (130g) raw pumpkin seeds, cleaned and dried
- 1 tablespoon (15ml) olive oil
- 1/2 teaspoon ground cumin
- 1/2 teaspoon smoked paprika
- 1/4 teaspoon chili powder
- 1/4 teaspoon garlic powder
- A pinch of cayenne pepper (optional for extra heat)
- Salt to taste

**INSTRUCTIONS:**

1. Preheat your oven to 350°F (175°C).
2. In a medium bowl, whisk together the olive oil, ground cumin, smoked paprika, chili powder, garlic powder, cayenne pepper, and salt.
3. After adding the pumpkin seeds to the bowl, toss them around to ensure they are well covered in the spice mixture.
4. Place the pumpkin seeds in a single layer on a baking sheet covered with parchment paper.
5. The seeds should be fragrant and brown after 15 to 20 minutes of baking in a preheated oven. Stir occasionally to ensure even roasting.
6. Once done, remove the seeds from the oven and let them cool. As the seeds cool, they will get crunchier.

**Nutritional Information (per serving):** • Calories: 193 kcal • Protein: 9g • Carbohydrates: 3g • Fat: 17g • Saturated Fat: 3g • Cholesterol: 0mg • Sodium: 5mg • Dietary Fiber: 2g • Sugars: 1g

## 2.8 Tuna Salad Stuffed Avocados

**Servings: 2 | Preparation Time: 15 minutes**

**INGREDIENTS:**

- 1 large ripe avocado, halved and pitted
- 1 can (5 ounces or 140g) tuna in water, drained and flaked
- 1/4 cup (60g) Greek yogurt, plain
- 2 tablespoons (30g) red onion, finely chopped
- 1/4 cup (30g) celery, finely chopped
- 1 tablespoon (15ml) lemon juice
- 1 teaspoon (5ml) Dijon mustard
- Salt and pepper to taste
- 1 tablespoon (15ml) fresh parsley, chopped (optional, for garnish)

**INSTRUCTIONS:**

1. Scoop out a small amount of avocado flesh from each half, being careful to leave a border so that the avocado looks like a "bowl." Chop the scooped avocado flesh and set aside.
2. In a medium bowl, mix the flaked tuna, Greek yogurt, chopped red onion, chopped celery, lemon juice, and Dijon mustard until well combined.
3. Fold in the chopped avocado bits. Add enough salt and pepper to taste while seasoning the mixture.
4. Evenly divide the tuna salad mixture between the avocado halves, stuffing them generously.
5. Garnish with fresh parsley if desired.

**Nutritional Information (per serving):**

• Calories: 290 kcal • Protein: 27g • Carbohydrates: 14g • Fat: 16g (Mono-unsaturated fat: 10g)
• Saturated Fat: 2.5g • Cholesterol: 25mg • Sodium: 200mg • Dietary Fiber: 7g • Sugars: 2g

# Chapter 3: Light Lunches

## 3.1 Tomato Basil Harmony Soup with Whole Wheat Croutons

**Servings: 2 | Total Time: 35 minutes**

### INGREDIENTS:

**For Tomato Basil Soup:**

- 2 tablespoons (30ml) olive oil
- 1/2 cup (60g) onion, finely chopped
- 2 cloves garlic, minced
- 1/2 teaspoon dried oregano
- 1/2 teaspoon dried basil
- 1/2 teaspoon dried thyme
- 1/2 teaspoon smoked paprika
- 1/2 teaspoon of optionally hot red pepper flakes
- 2 cans (14 oz / 400g each) diced tomatoes, undrained
- 2 cups (480ml) vegetable broth
- Salt and black pepper, to taste
- Fresh basil leaves for garnish

**For Whole Wheat Croutons:**

- 2 slices whole wheat bread, cubed
- 2 teaspoons olive oil
- 1/2 teaspoon garlic powder
- 1/2 teaspoon dried oregano
- Pinch of salt

### INSTRUCTIONS:

**For Tomato Basil Soup:**

1. Heat the olive oil in a large pot over medium heat. Add the onions and garlic, sautéing until the onions are translucent, about 5 minutes.
2. Stir in the dried oregano, dried basil, dried thyme, smoked paprika, and red pepper flakes (if using). Cook for another 1-2 minutes until the mixture is fragrant.
3. Add the undrained diced tomatoes and vegetable broth. Bring to a boil, then simmer for 20 to 25 minutes to allow the flavors to meld.
4. Gently transfer the soup to a blender and blend until smooth, or use an immersion blender directly in the pot.
5. If you used a blender, return the soup to the pot and season with salt and black pepper to taste. Keep warm while preparing the croutons.

**For Whole Wheat Croutons:**

1. Preheat the oven to 375°F (190°C). Alternatively, you can use a skillet for toasting.
2. In a bowl, toss the cubed whole wheat bread with olive oil, garlic powder, dried oregano, and a pinch of salt until evenly coated.
3. Spread the seasoned bread cubes on a baking sheet and bake for 10 to 15 minutes, or toast in a skillet until crisp and golden brown, stirring occasionally for even browning.

**Assemble and Serve:**

1. Ladle the Tomato Basil Harmony Soup into bowls.
2. Top each with a generous amount of whole wheat croutons.
3. Garnish with fresh basil leaves just before serving.

**Nutritional Information (per serving):**

• Calories: 947 • Fat: 62.2g • Saturated Fat: 9.6g • Cholesterol: 0mg • Sodium: 10401mg • Carbohydrate: 98.55g • Fiber: 31.45g • Protein: 22.35g

# 3.2 Rainbow Salad with Lemon Tahini Dressing

**Servings: 2 | Preparation Time: 15 minutes**

## INGREDIENTS:

### For the Rainbow Salad:

- 2 cups (60g) mixed salad greens (spinach, arugula, romaine)
- 1/2 cup (75g) cherry tomatoes, halved
- 1 small carrot, julienned
- 1/4 red bell pepper, thinly sliced
- 1/4 yellow bell pepper, thinly sliced
- 1/4 cucumber, thinly sliced
- 1/4 small red onion, thinly sliced
- 1/4 cup (30g) red cabbage, shredded
- 1/4 cup (50g) cooked and cooled quinoa
- 2 tablespoons (20g) walnuts, chopped (optional)

### For the Lemon Tahini Dressing:

- 3 tablespoons (45g) tahini
- 2 tablespoons (30ml) lemon juice
- 1 tablespoon (15ml) olive oil
- 1 clove garlic, minced
- 2-3 tablespoons water (to thin)
- Salt and pepper to taste
- Optional: 1 teaspoon honey or maple syrup for a touch of sweetness

## INSTRUCTIONS:

### For the Rainbow Salad:

1. Mix the mixed salad greens, cherry tomatoes, julienned carrots, sliced cucumber, sliced red onion, shredded red cabbage, sliced red and yellow bell peppers, and chilled quinoa in a large salad dish.
2. Toss the salad components gently to mix them evenly.

### For the Lemon Tahini Dressing:

1. Combine the tahini, olive oil, lemon juice, and minced garlic in a small bowl and whisk until smooth.
2. Gradually add water, one tablespoon at a time, until the dressing reaches your preferred consistency.
3. Taste and adjust the dressing with salt and pepper. For a little sweetness, feel free to add honey or maple syrup and stir once more.

### To Serve:

1. Drizzle the Lemon Tahini Dressing over the prepared salad.
2. Toss until the dressing coats every component equally.
3. Sprinkle with chopped walnuts if you're including them for an added texture and omega-3 fatty acids, which are great for heart health.
4. Enjoy the vibrant explosion of tastes and colors as you divide the salad into two servings.

### Nutritional Information (per serving):

- Calories: 315 kcal • Protein: 10g • Carbohydrates: 23g • Fat: 22g • Saturated Fat: 3g • Cholesterol: 0mg
- Sodium: 70mg • Dietary Fiber: 6g • Sugars: 5g

# 3.3 Grilled Vegetable Panini with Pesto

Servings: 2 | Total Time: 30 minutes

## INGREDIENTS:

### For the Panini:

- 4 slices whole-grain bread
- 1 small zucchini, sliced lengthwise into thin strips
- 1 small yellow squash, sliced lengthwise into thin strips
- 1/2 red bell pepper, cut into thin strips
- 1/2 red onion, cut into rings
- 1 tablespoon (15ml) olive oil
- Salt and pepper, to taste
- 4 tablespoons fresh pesto sauce (store-bought or homemade)
- 4 slices reduced-fat mozzarella cheese

### For the Pesto:

- 1 cup (40g) fresh basil leaves
- 2 cloves garlic
- 3 tablespoons (45ml) olive oil
- 2 tablespoons (30g) grated Parmesan cheese
- 1 tablespoon (15g) pine nuts (optional)
- Salt, to taste

## INSTRUCTIONS:

**For the Pesto (if making your own):** Place the basil leaves, garlic, olive oil, grated Parmesan cheese, and pine nuts (if using) into a food processor or blender. Add extra olive oil to the blender if needed to get the required consistency when it's smooth. Season with salt to taste.

### Grilling the Vegetables:

1. Preheat your grill or grill pan over medium heat.
2. Toss zucchini, yellow squash, red bell pepper, and onion rings with olive oil, salt, and pepper.
3. The vegetables should be soft and have lovely grill marks after grilling for around 4–5 minutes on each side.

### Assembling the Panini:

1. Spread each slice of whole-grain bread with 1 tablespoon of pesto sauce.
2. Layer the grilled vegetables on two of the bread slices.
3. Top the veggies with 2 slices of mozzarella cheese.
4. To finish the sandwiches, place the remaining bread slices on top, pesto side down.

### Grilling the Panini:

1. Over medium heat, preheat a grill pan or Panini press. If using a grill pan, you can press the Panini with a heavy skillet on top.
2. Grill the sandwich for 3-5 minutes on each side or until the cheese has melted and the bread is crispy.

## Nutritional Information (per serving):

• Calories: 500 kcal • Protein: 18g • Carbohydrates: 35g • Fat: 34g • Saturated Fat: 8g • Cholesterol: 20mg
• Sodium: 790mg • Dietary Fiber: 5g • Sugars: 7g

## 3.4 Chickpea and Cucumber Salad

**Servings: 2 | Preparation Time: 15 minutes**

**INGREDIENTS:**

- 1 cup (240g) chickpeas, drained and rinsed
- 1 large cucumber, diced
- 1/2 red onion, finely chopped
- 1/2 bell pepper (any color), diced
- 10 cherry tomatoes, halved
- 2 tablespoons fresh parsley, chopped
- 2 tablespoons olive oil
- 1 tablespoon lemon juice
- 1 clove garlic, minced
- Salt and pepper to taste
- 1/4 teaspoon ground cumin (optional)
- 2 tablespoons crumbled feta cheese (optional for extra flavor)

**INSTRUCTIONS:**

1. Chickpeas that have been rinsed and drained should be combined with sliced cucumber, diced bell pepper, diced red onion, and split cherry tomatoes in a big bowl.
2. To make the dressing, combine the ground cumin (if using), olive oil, lemon juice, chopped garlic, salt, and pepper in a small bowl.
3. Once the salad's ingredients are fully coated, pour the dressing over them and toss again.
4. Add the chopped fresh parsley and feta cheese (if using) to the salad and gently mix to incorporate.
5. To enable the flavors to mingle, cover and refrigerate the salad for at least 10 minutes.
6. Serve cold as a wholesome and revitalizing side dish.

**Nutritional Information (per serving):**

• Calories: 275 kcal • Protein: 9g • Carbohydrates: 29g • Fat: 14g • Saturated Fat: 2g (if using feta)

• Cholesterol: 0mg (8mg if using feta) • Sodium: 200mg (320mg if using feta) • Dietary Fiber: 8g • Sugars: 6g

## 3.5 Whole Grain Tabbouleh

**Servings: 2 | Preparation Time: 25 minutes (plus chilling time)**

**INGREDIENTS:**

- 1/2 cup (90g) bulgur wheat
- 1 cup (240ml) boiling water
- 1 cup (30g) fresh parsley, finely chopped
- 1/4 cup (10g) fresh mint, finely chopped
- 2 medium tomatoes, diced
- 1/2 cucumber, seeded and diced
- 1/4 red onion, finely diced
- 2 tablespoons (30ml) lemon juice
- 1 tablespoon (15ml) extra virgin olive oil
- Salt and pepper, to taste

**INSTRUCTIONS:**

1. The bulgur wheat should be put in a big bowl. Cover the bulgur with boiling water, then leave it for ten to fifteen minutes, or until the bulgur has absorbed the water and become soft.

2. Once the bulgur has cooled to room temperature, fluff it with a fork.
3. Add the finely chopped parsley, mint, diced tomatoes, diced cucumber, and red onion to the bulgur.
4. Make the dressing by whisking the olive oil and lemon juice in a small bowl and adding salt and pepper to taste.
5. Pour the dressing over the bulgur and vegetable mixture and toss until well combined.
6. To let the flavors combine, cover and chill the tabbouleh for at least an hour.
7. Before serving, give the tabbouleh a final toss and adjust the seasoning if necessary.

### Nutritional Information (per serving):
• Calories: 220 kcal • Protein: 6g • Carbohydrates: 42g • Fat: 5g • Saturated Fat: 0.5g • Cholesterol: 0mg
• Sodium: 10mg • Dietary Fiber: 10g • Sugars: 3g

---

## 3.6 Curried Lentil Soup

**Servings: 2 | Total Time: 45 minutes**

### INGREDIENTS:

- 1/2 cup (100g) dried green or brown lentils, rinsed
- 2 tablespoons (30ml) olive oil
- 1/2 cup (60g) onion, finely chopped
- 2 cloves garlic, minced
- 1/2 cup (60g) carrot, diced
- 1/2 cup (60g) celery, diced
- 1/2 teaspoon ground cumin
- 1/2 teaspoon ground coriander
- 1/2 teaspoon smoked paprika
- 1/2 teaspoon dried thyme
- Salt and black pepper, to taste
- 4 cups (960ml) vegetable broth
- 1 cup (120g) fresh spinach leaves, chopped
- 2 tablespoons (30ml) lemon juice (optional)

### INSTRUCTIONS:
1. Rinse dried lentils under cold water.
2. Heat the olive oil in a pot of moderate size. Add chopped onion and garlic, sautéing until fragrant and translucent.
3. Add the diced carrot, celery, smoked paprika, ground coriander, cumin, dried thyme, salt, and black pepper and stir.
4. Add rinsed lentils to the pot and stir to combine with the vegetables and spices.
5. Pour vegetable broth into the pot, bringing the mixture to a gentle boil.
6. Reduce heat to low, cover, and let the soup simmer for about 20-25 minutes or until lentils are tender.
7. Stir in chopped fresh spinach and let it wilt into the soup.
8. After tasting the soup, adjust the seasoning. Add more salt or pepper if desired.
9. If desired, squeeze lemon juice into the soup for a refreshing kick.

### Nutritional Information (per serving):
• Calories: 742 • Fat: 54.3g • Saturated Fat: 8.3g • Cholesterol: 0mg • Sodium: 424mg • Carbohydrate: 64.9g
• Fiber: 21.3g • Protein: 17.6g • Sugars: Not Specified

# 3.7 Asian Chicken Lettuce Wraps

Servings: 2 | Preparation Time: 20 minutes | Cooking Time: 15 minutes

**INGREDIENTS:**

- 2 large chicken breasts (approximately 200g each), diced into small pieces
- 1 tablespoon (15ml) sesame oil
- 1 cup (128g) shiitake mushrooms, finely chopped
- 1/2 cup (64g) water chestnuts, diced
- 1 small carrot, julienned
- 1 tablespoon (15ml) low-sodium soy sauce
- 1 tablespoon (15ml) hoisin sauce
- 1 teaspoon (5ml) rice vinegar
- 1 clove garlic, minced
- 1 teaspoon fresh ginger, grated
- 1/4 teaspoon red pepper flakes (optional, adjust to taste)
- 4-6 large lettuce leaves (such as Iceberg or Butter lettuce)
- Fresh cilantro for garnish
- Optional garnishes: green onions, sesame seeds

**INSTRUCTIONS:**

1. Over medium heat, preheat sesame oil in a large skillet. Add the diced chicken and heat, tossing regularly, until the chicken is no longer pink in the center.

2. Once the chicken is cooked through, add the shiitake mushrooms, water chestnuts, and julienned carrot to the skillet. Cook for an additional 2-3 minutes until the vegetables are tender but still crunchy.

3. To make the sauce, combine the low-sodium soy sauce, hoisin sauce, rice vinegar, grated ginger, chopped garlic, and red pepper flakes (if using) in a small bowl.

4. Pour the sauce over the skillet's contents, making sure to coat every piece of chicken and vegetable mixture. Cook for another 2-3 minutes, stirring frequently to allow the flavors to combine.

5. After washing and patting dry, place a spoonful of the chicken mixture in the middle of each lettuce leaf.

6. Garnish with fresh cilantro, green onions, and sesame seeds, if desired, before serving.

**Nutritional Information (per serving):**

• Calories: 295 kcal • Protein: 34g • Carbohydrates: 10g • Fat: 13g • Saturated Fat: 2g • Cholesterol: 82mg
• Sodium: 450mg • Dietary Fiber: 2g • Sugars: 5g

# Chapter 4: Satisfying Salads

## 4.1 Walnut and Beet Salad with Citrus Vinaigrette

**Servings: 2 | Preparation Time: 15 minutes (plus time for roasting beets if fresh)**

### INGREDIENTS:

- 2 medium beets, roasted, peeled, and diced
- 1/2 cup (50g) walnuts, roughly chopped
- 4 cups (120g) mixed salad greens (such as baby spinach, arugula)
- 1/4 cup (30g) crumbled goat cheese or feta cheese (optional)
- 1 small orange, peeled and segmented
- 2 tablespoons (30ml) extra virgin olive oil
- 1 tablespoon (15ml) orange juice
- 1 tablespoon (15ml) lemon juice
- 1 teaspoon (5ml) honey
- 1 teaspoon (5ml) Dijon mustard
- Salt and pepper to taste

### INSTRUCTIONS:

1. If using fresh beets, preheat your oven to 400°F (200°C), wrap beets in foil, and roast for about 45-60 minutes until tender. Once cooled, peel and dice them.
2. Combine the mixed salad greens in a large serving bowl.
3. Add the diced beets and walnut pieces to the greens and toss lightly.
4. To prepare the citrus vinaigrette, whisk together the olive oil, orange juice, lemon juice, honey, and Dijon mustard in a small bowl. To taste, add more salt and pepper for seasoning.
5. Over the salad, drizzle with the vinaigrette and toss until all the elements are evenly coated.
6. Top with the orange segments and crumbled goat cheese or feta cheese if desired.
7. Serve the salad immediately, garnished with any additional walnuts or a sprinkle of extra cheese.

### Nutritional Information (per serving):

• Calories: 360 kcal • Protein: 9g • Carbohydrates: 20g • Fat: 29g • Saturated Fat: 4g • Cholesterol: 10mg
• Sodium: 250mg • Dietary Fiber: 5g • Sugars: 12g

## 4.2 Spinach, Strawberry, and Quinoa Salad

Servings: 2 | Preparation Time: 20 minutes | Cooking Time: Quinoa – according to package directions

### INGREDIENTS:

- 1 cup (160g) quinoa, cooked and cooled
- 4 cups (120g) fresh spinach leaves, rinsed and dried
- 1 cup (152g) strawberries, hulled and sliced
- 1/4 cup (30g) sliced almonds
- 2 tablespoons (10g) crumbled feta or goat cheese (optional)
- 2 tablespoons (30ml) balsamic vinegar
- 1 tablespoon (15ml) extra virgin olive oil
- 1 teaspoon (7g) honey
- A pinch of salt and freshly ground pepper to taste

### INSTRUCTIONS:

1. Prepare the quinoa according to the package instructions. Allow it to cool.
2. In a large bowl, mix the fresh spinach leaves with the cooled quinoa.
3. Add the sliced strawberries and almonds to the salad and gently toss.
4. For the dressing, whisk together balsamic vinegar, extra virgin olive oil, honey, salt, and pepper in a small bowl until well-combined.
5. After adding the dressing, toss the salad one more to make sure everything is well coated.
6. If you're using goat cheese or feta, crumble it on top to add some richness and taste.
7. Serve immediately, offering extra dressing on the side if needed.

**Nutritional Information (per serving):**

• Calories: 345 kcal • Protein: 12g • Carbohydrates: 45g • Fat: 14g • Saturated Fat: 2g • Cholesterol: 8mg
• Sodium: 200mg • Dietary Fiber: 7g • Sugars: 8g

## 4.3 Kale Caesar with Spelt Croutons

Servings: 2 | Preparation Time: 25 minutes | Cooking Time: 15 minutes for croutons

### INGREDIENTS:

- 4 cups (134g) fresh kale leaves, stems removed and leaves chopped
- 1/2 cup (74g) spelt bread, cut into 1/2-inch cubes
- 1 tablespoon (15ml) olive oil
- 1/4 teaspoon (1.25g) garlic powder
- Salt and pepper to taste

**For the Caesar Dressing:**
- 1/4 cup (60ml) low-fat Greek yogurt
- 1 tablespoon (15ml) lemon juice
- 1 small garlic clove, minced
- 1 teaspoon (5ml) Dijon mustard
- 1 teaspoon (2g) anchovy paste (optional)
- 1 tablespoon (15ml) Parmesan cheese, grated
- 1 tablespoon (15ml) water (or more to thin the dressing)
- Salt and pepper to taste

## INSTRUCTIONS:

1. Preheat the oven to 375°F (190°C) for the spelt croutons.
2. The spelt bread cubes should be equally coated after being tossed in a basin with olive oil, salt, pepper, and garlic powder.
3. After arranging the bread cubes on a baking sheet, bake them for 10-15 minutes, rotating them halfway through, or until they are crisp and browned.
4. While the croutons are baking, wash and chop the kale leaves, making sure to remove the stems.
5. For the Caesar dressing, combine Greek yogurt, lemon juice, minced garlic, Dijon mustard, anchovy paste (if using), and grated Parmesan cheese in a bowl. Add water as necessary to achieve the required consistency and whisk until smooth. Season with salt and pepper to taste.
6. In a large salad bowl, massage the dressing into the kale leaves until the leaves are coated and tenderized.
7. Add the baked spelt croutons to the dressed kale and toss lightly.
8. Serve the salad with a sprinkle of additional Parmesan cheese if desired.

### Nutritional Information (per serving):

• Calories: 270 kcal • Protein: 13g • Carbohydrates: 35g • Fat: 11g • Saturated Fat: 2g • Cholesterol: 5mg
• Sodium: 350mg • Dietary Fiber: 4g • Sugars: 3g

## 4.4 Broccoli Slaw with Ginger Peanut Dressing

**Servings: 2 | Preparation Time: 20 minutes**

### INGREDIENTS:

• 2 cups (250g) broccoli slaw (shredded broccoli stems, carrots, and red cabbage)
• 1/4 cup (30g) red bell pepper, thinly sliced
• 2 green onions, sliced
• 2 tablespoons (16g) unsalted roasted peanuts, roughly chopped
• 2 tablespoons (30ml) cilantro, chopped (optional)

### For the Ginger Peanut Dressing:

• 2 tablespoons (32g) natural peanut butter
• 1 tablespoon (15ml) low-sodium soy sauce
• 1 tablespoon (15ml) rice vinegar
• 1 tablespoon (15ml) water
• 1 teaspoon (2g) fresh ginger, grated
• 1 small garlic clove, minced
• 1 teaspoon (5ml) honey or maple syrup
• A pinch of red pepper flakes (optional)

### INSTRUCTIONS:

1. Toss the red bell pepper, green onions, and prepared broccoli slaw mix in a large salad dish.
2. To make the dressing, whisk together the peanut butter, soy sauce, rice vinegar, water, grated ginger, minced garlic, honey or maple syrup, and red pepper flakes in a small bowl until smooth and thoroughly combined.
3. Pour the ginger peanut dressing over the slaw mixture and toss until well-coated.
4. Garnish with chopped peanuts and fresh cilantro if desired.
5. Serve immediately, or let the salad chill in the refrigerator for an hour to allow the flavors to meld.

### Nutritional Information (per serving):

• Calories: 210 kcal • Protein: 8g • Carbohydrates: 18g • Fat: 13g • Saturated Fat: 2g • Cholesterol: 0mg
• Sodium: 320mg • Dietary Fiber: 5g • Sugars: 7g

## 4.5 Grilled Peach and Burrata Salad

Servings: 2 | Preparation Time: 15 minutes | Cooking Time: 6-8 minutes for peaches

### INGREDIENTS:

- 2 ripe peaches, halved and pitted
- 1 tablespoon (15ml) olive oil
- 4 cups (120g) mixed salad greens, such as arugula and spinach
- 1 ball (4oz / 113g) burrata cheese
- A handful of fresh basil leaves, torn
- Balsamic glaze for drizzling
- Salt and freshly ground pepper to taste

### INSTRUCTIONS:

1. Preheat the grill to medium-high heat.
2. To keep the peach halves from sticking to the grill, lightly coat them with olive oil.
3. Place peach halves onto the grill, cut side down, and cook for 3-4 minutes until you see grill marks. After turning the peaches over, grill them for a further 3-4 minutes, or until they are soft but not mushy.
4. Divide the mixed salad greens between two plates or arrange them on a serving dish.
5. When the peaches are done, let them cool for a minute and then arrange them on top of the greens.
6. Place the burrata cheese in the center of the greens and gently tear it open to let the creamy inside mingle with the salad.
7. Sprinkle shredded basil leaves over the salad and drizzle with balsamic glaze. To taste, add freshly ground pepper and salt.
8. Serve immediately and enjoy the symphony of warm, sweet peaches and cool, creamy burrata with the tang of the balsamic and the peppery salad greens.

### Nutritional Information (per serving):

• Calories: 370 kcal • Protein: 18g • Carbohydrates: 20g • Fat: 25g • Saturated Fat: 11g • Cholesterol: 40mg • Sodium: 400mg • Dietary Fiber: 3g • Sugars: 17g

## 4.6 Caprese Salad with Balsamic Reduction

Servings: 2 | Preparation Time: 10 minutes | Reduction Cooking Time: 10-15 minutes

### INGREDIENTS:

- 2 large ripe tomatoes, sliced
- 1 ball (8oz / 226g) fresh mozzarella cheese, sliced
- Fresh basil leaves
- 1/4 cup (60ml) balsamic vinegar
- 1 tablespoon (15ml) extra virgin olive oil
- Salt and freshly ground black pepper to taste

### INSTRUCTIONS:

1. Transfer the balsamic vinegar to a small saucepan and set it over medium-low heat to make the balsamic reduction.
2. Bring the vinegar to a simmer and, occasionally whisking, reduce it by half and thicken, which should take 10-15 minutes. Be careful not to over-reduce it, or it will become too thick. Let the reduction cool to room temperature; it will thicken as it cools.

3. Arrange the tomato slices, mozzarella cheese slices, and fresh basil leaves in a tiered fashion on a serving dish.

4. Drizzle the tomatoes, mozzarella, and basil with the extra virgin olive oil.

5. Toss in the salad and season with salt and freshly ground black pepper.

6. Drizzle the Caprese salad with the balsamic reduction right before serving.

7. Serve this classic Italian salad as a refreshing appetizer or as a light and elegant lunch.

**Nutritional Information (per serving):**

• Calories: 380 kcal • Protein: 22g • Carbohydrates: 14g • Fat: 27g • Saturated Fat: 12g • Cholesterol: 60mg • Sodium: 540mg • Dietary Fiber: 2g • Sugars: 10g

## 4.7 Mixed Greens with Roasted Sweet Potato & Pecans

**Servings: 2 | Preparation Time: 15 minutes | Cooking Time: 25 minutes**

**INGREDIENTS:**

• 1 large sweet potato, peeled and cubed (about 2 cups)
• 1 tablespoon (15ml) olive oil
• Salt and pepper to taste
• 4 cups (120g) mixed salad greens, such as baby spinach, arugula, and romaine
• 1/4 cup (30g) pecans, toasted and roughly chopped
• Optional enhancements: dried cranberries, goat cheese, or sliced red onions

**For the Vinaigrette:**

• 2 tablespoons (30ml) extra virgin olive oil
• 1 tablespoon (15ml) apple cider vinegar
• 1 teaspoon (5ml) Dijon mustard
• 1 teaspoon (5ml) honey or maple syrup
• Salt and pepper to taste

**INSTRUCTIONS:**

1. Preheat the oven to 400°F (200°C). Add salt and pepper to the diced sweet potatoes after tossing them in olive oil. Place them in a single layer on a baking sheet and roast for 25 minutes, stirring occasionally, or until they are tender and have a hint of caramelization.

2. As the sweet potatoes are roasting, make the vinaigrette by combining the apple cider vinegar, honey, maple syrup, and extra virgin olive oil in a small bowl. Season with salt and pepper to taste.

3. Heat a dry skillet over medium heat and toast the nuts, being careful not to burn them until they become fragrant and lightly browned.

4. Place the mixed salad greens in a large bowl. Add the roasted sweet potatoes and toasted pecans. If you're using any optional ingredients, add them now.

5. Over the salad, drizzle the prepared vinaigrette and gently toss to coat evenly.

6. Divide the salad between two plates, serve, and enjoy this hearty, nutritious, and flavorful dish.

**Nutritional Information (per serving):**

• Calories: 380 kcal • Protein: 5g • Carbohydrates: 30g • Fat: 29g • Saturated Fat: 3g • Cholesterol: 0mg • Sodium: 200mg • Dietary Fiber: 6g • Sugars: 9g

# 4.8 Farro and Roasted Vegetable Salad

Servings: 2 | Preparation Time: 15 minutes | Cooking Time: ~30 minutes

## INGREDIENTS:

- 1 cup (200g) farro, rinsed
- 2 cups (about 240g) assorted vegetables (e.g., bell peppers, zucchini, carrots, and onion), chopped into bite-sized pieces
- 2 tablespoons (30ml) extra virgin olive oil, divided
- Salt and freshly ground black pepper to taste
- 2 tablespoons (30ml) red wine vinegar
- 1 garlic clove, minced
- 1 teaspoon (5ml) honey or maple syrup
- 1/4 cup (10g) fresh parsley, finely chopped
- Optional add-ins: feta cheese, chickpeas, or cherry tomatoes

## INSTRUCTIONS:

1. Preheat the oven to 400°F (200°C).
2. Heat 3 cups of water in a medium-sized pot until it boils. Add the rinsed farro, reduce the heat to a simmer, and cook for 25-30 minutes, or until the farro is tender but still chewy. After removing any extra water, leave it to cool.
3. Add salt, pepper, and one tablespoon of olive oil to the chopped vegetables. Place the vegetables in a single layer on a baking sheet and bake in a preheated oven for 20 to 25 minutes, turning the pan halfway through, or until the vegetables are tender and browned.
4. Combine the red wine vinegar, honey or maple syrup, minced garlic, and the remaining olive oil in a small bowl to create the vinaigrette. Season with salt and black pepper.
5. The cooked farro, roasted veggies, and fresh parsley should all be combined in a big bowl. If using any optional add-ins, fold those into the salad now.
6. Drizzle the salad with the vinaigrette and thoroughly mix to incorporate.
7. Serve this rustic and hearty farro salad warm or at room temperature.

## Nutritional Information (per serving):

• Calories: 540 kcal • Protein: 12g • Carbohydrates: 78g • Fat: 22g • Saturated Fat: 3g • Cholesterol: 0mg
• Sodium: 300mg • Dietary Fiber: 15g • Sugars: 8g

# Chapter 5: Hearty Soups and Stews

## 5.1 Lentil and Vegetable Stew

Servings: 2 | Preparation Time: 10 minutes | Cooking Time: 35-40 minutes

### INGREDIENTS:

- 1/2 cup (100g) dried green or brown lentils, rinsed
- 1 tablespoon (15ml) olive oil
- 1/4 cup (30g) onion, finely chopped
- 1 clove garlic, minced
- 1/4 cup (30g) carrot, diced
- 1/4 cup (30g) celery, diced
- 1/4 teaspoon ground cumin
- 1/4 teaspoon ground coriander
- 1/4 teaspoon smoked paprika
- 1/4 teaspoon dried thyme
- Salt and freshly ground black pepper, to taste
- 2 cups (480ml) vegetable broth
- 1/2 cup (60g) fresh spinach leaves, chopped
- 1 tablespoon (15ml) lemon juice (optional)

### INSTRUCTIONS:

1. Begin by rinsing the dried lentils under cold water to remove any impurities.
2. In a pot that is medium in size, warm the olive oil. Add the chopped onion and garlic, and sauté until they turn fragrant and translucent.
3. Add the diced carrot and celery, salt, black pepper, smoked paprika, ground coriander, cumin, and dried thyme. Cook for a few minutes.
4. Stir everything well to incorporate after adding the rinsed lentils to the pot.
5. Once the vegetable broth has been added to the pot, turn up the heat so that the mixture gently boils.
6. When the stew reaches a boil, lower the heat to a simmer, cover the pot, and allow the stew to cook for about 25 minutes or until the lentils are soft.
7. Add the chopped fresh spinach to the pot, stirring through until wilted.
8. If extra salt or pepper is wanted, taste the stew and adjust the seasoning accordingly.
9. If you're using lemon juice, squeeze it into the stew before serving for a zesty kick.
10. Transfer the stew into bowls and serve it warm, maybe accompanied by a crusty bread slice.

### Nutritional Information (per serving):

• Calories: 342 kcal • Protein: 17.6g • Carbohydrates: 64.95g • Fat: 54.35g • Saturated Fat: 8.35g

• Cholesterol: 0mg • Sodium: 424mg • Dietary Fiber: 21.3g • Sugars: 3.5g

## 5.2 Tomato and Red Pepper Gazpacho

Servings: 2 | Preparation Time: 15 minutes | No Cooking Required

### INGREDIENTS:

- 3 large ripe tomatoes, roughly chopped
- 1 red bell pepper, seeded and roughly chopped
- 1/2 cucumber, peeled and roughly chopped
- 1/4 red onion, peeled and roughly chopped
- 1 clove garlic, minced
- 2 tablespoons (30ml) extra virgin olive oil
- 1 tablespoon (15ml) red wine vinegar
- Salt and freshly ground black pepper, to taste
- 1/2 teaspoon smoked paprika
- A pinch of cayenne pepper (optional for a spicy kick)
- Fresh basil or parsley leaves for garnish
- 1/4 cup (60ml) cold water or vegetable broth, if needed for consistency

### INSTRUCTIONS:

1. Add the chopped tomatoes, red bell pepper, cucumber, red onion, and minced garlic to a food processor or blender.
2. Toss in the extra virgin olive oil, red wine vinegar, smoked paprika, black pepper, salt, and cayenne (if using).
3. Blend the mixture until the appropriate consistency is achieved. If you prefer a thinner gazpacho, you may add cold water or vegetable broth to adjust it.
4. After tasting the gazpacho, adjust the seasoning by adding additional vinegar, salt, or pepper as necessary.
5. Place the gazpacho in the fridge and let it get cold, preferably for at least an hour. This step is important as the flavors meld and intensify during this time.
6. Serve the chilled gazpacho in bowls or glasses, garnished with fresh basil or parsley leaves.

Nutritional Information (per serving): • Calories: 171 kcal • Protein: 3g • Carbohydrates: 17g • Fat: 11g • Saturated Fat: 1.5g • Cholesterol: 0mg • Sodium: 12mg • Dietary Fiber: 5g • Sugars: 10g

## 5.3 Carrot and Ginger Soup with Coconut

Servings: 2 | Preparation Time: 10 minutes | Cooking Time: 25-30 minutes

### INGREDIENTS:

- 4 large carrots, peeled and sliced
- 1 tablespoon (15ml) olive oil or coconut oil
- 1 small onion, chopped
- 2 cloves garlic, minced
- 2 teaspoons (10ml) fresh ginger, grated
- 1/4 teaspoon ground turmeric
- Salt and fresh ground black pepper, to taste
- 2 cups (480ml) low-sodium vegetable broth
- 1/2 cup (120ml) canned light coconut milk
- Fresh coriander (cilantro) or parsley for garnish
- Optional: pumpkin seeds or coconut flakes for garnish

## INSTRUCTIONS:

1. In a large pot set over medium heat, warm the coconut oil or olive oil. Add the chopped onions and simmer for 3–4 minutes, or until they are transparent.
2. Cook for an additional 1-2 minutes, or until aromatic, after adding the grated ginger and minced garlic.
3. Add the sliced carrots to the pot, along with the ground turmeric, and season with salt and pepper. Cook for 5 minutes, stirring occasionally.
4. After adding the veggie broth, heat the mixture until it boils. After that, lower the heat, cover, and boil the carrots for about 20 minutes, or until they are soft.
5. Take off the heat and add the coconut milk, mixing everything until it's creamy. You can use an immersion blender for convenience or carefully transfer the soup to a stand blender.
6. Taste and adjust seasoning if necessary. To get the right consistency, thin up any extra soup by adding a small amount of broth or water.
7. Serve the soup warm, garnished with fresh coriander (cilantro) and optional pumpkin seeds or coconut flakes.

**Nutritional Information (per serving):** • Calories: 234 kcal • Protein: 3g • Carbohydrates: 19g • Fat: 17g • Saturated Fat: 12g • Cholesterol: 0mg • Sodium: 506mg • Dietary Fiber: 5g • Sugars: 9g

## 5.4 Rustic Potato Leek Soup

**Servings: 2 | Preparation Time: 15 minutes | Cooking Time: 30 minutes**

### INGREDIENTS:

- 2 large potatoes (about 400g), peeled and diced
- 1 tablespoon (15ml) olive oil
- 2 leeks, white and light green parts only, sliced and cleaned thoroughly
- 1 clove garlic, minced
- 1/4 teaspoon dried thyme
- Salt and freshly ground black pepper, to taste
- 3 cups (720ml) low-sodium vegetable broth
- Optional: 1/4 cup (60ml) low-fat milk or unsweetened almond milk for creaminess
- Optional: chives or parsley for garnish

### INSTRUCTIONS:

1. The olive oil should be heated to a medium temperature in a big pot. Add the sliced leeks and cook, stirring occasionally, until they are soft and translucent, about 7-8 minutes.
2. Add the minced garlic to the leeks and cook for another minute until fragrant.
3. Stir in the diced potatoes, dried thyme, salt, and pepper, and cook for a few minutes, making sure to coat the potatoes well with the leek and spice mixture.
4. After adding the veggie broth, heat the soup until it boils. After that, cover the saucepan and reduce the heat to a simmer.
5. The potatoes should be soft and easily punctured with a fork after about 20 minutes of cooking.
6. For a rustic texture, you can use a potato masher to gently mash some of the potatoes in the pot. To achieve a smoother soup, carefully combine the hot liquid in small batches using an immersion blender or a regular blender.
7. To give a little smoothness, whisk in the almond milk or low-fat milk, if using, then taste and adjust the spice.
8. Serve the soup warm, garnished with chopped chives or parsley, if desired.

**Nutritional Information (per serving):** • Calories: 287 kcal • Protein: 6g • Carbohydrates: 51g • Fat: 7g

• Saturated Fat: 1g • Cholesterol: 1mg • Sodium: 84mg • Dietary Fiber: 6g • Sugars: 5g

# 5.5 Spicy Black Bean Soup

Servings: 2 | Preparation Time: 10 minutes | Cooking Time: 25 minutes

## INGREDIENTS:

- 2 cups (400g) black beans, cooked and drained
- 1 tablespoon (15ml) olive oil
- 1 small onion, diced
- 2 cloves garlic, minced
- 1 teaspoon ground cumin
- 1/2 teaspoon chili powder
- 1/4 teaspoon smoked paprika
- 1 small jalapeño pepper, seeded and diced (optional for extra heat)
- 3 cups (720ml) low-sodium vegetable broth
- Salt and freshly ground black pepper, to taste
- Optional: lime wedges, diced red onion, chopped cilantro, and avocado for topping

## INSTRUCTIONS:

1. In a pot that is medium in size, warm the olive oil. Add the chopped onion and simmer for three to five minutes, or until it is soft and transparent.
2. Stir in the minced garlic, ground cumin, chili powder, smoked paprika, and diced jalapeño (if using). Cook until fragrant, about 1 minute.
3. After the black beans are cooked, add the vegetable broth to the pot.
4. Once the soup reaches a boiling point, lower the heat to a simmer. To let the flavors mingle, partially cover the pot and simmer for about 20 minutes.
5. If you would like to have the soup chunkier, feel free to purée it with an immersion blender to your preferred consistency.
6. Use salt and black pepper to adjust the seasoning based on taste. You can thin out an overly thick soup by adding extra stock.
7. Serve the soup hot, with optional toppings such as a squeeze of lime juice, diced red onion, chopped cilantro, and slices of avocado.

## Nutritional Information (per serving):

• Calories: 345 kcal • Protein: 18g • Carbohydrates: 52g • Fat: 7g • Saturated Fat: 1g • Cholesterol: 0mg

• Sodium: 500mg • Dietary Fiber: 13g • Sugars: 2g

# Chapter 6: Main Dish Magic

## 6.1 Ratatouille with Baked Polenta

Servings: 2 | Preparation Time: 15 minutes | Cooking Time: 40 minutes

### INGREDIENTS:

**For the Ratatouille:**

- 1 small zucchini, sliced into rounds
- 1 small yellow squash, sliced into rounds
- 1 small eggplant, cubed
- 1 bell pepper (any color), deseeded and chopped
- 2 medium tomatoes, chopped
- 1/2 onion, chopped
- 2 cloves garlic, minced
- 2 tablespoons (30ml) olive oil
- 1 teaspoon (5ml) dried thyme
- 1 teaspoon (5ml) dried basil
- Salt and freshly ground black pepper, to taste

**For the Polenta:**

- 1/2 cup (70g) polenta (coarse cornmeal)
- 2 cups (480ml) water or vegetable broth
- Pinch of salt
- 1 tablespoon (14g) unsalted butter or olive oil (optional, for richness)

### INSTRUCTIONS:

**For the Ratatouille:**

1. Preheat the oven to 375°F (190°C).
2. In a large bowl, combine zucchini, yellow squash, eggplant, bell pepper, tomatoes, onion, and garlic. Toss with olive oil, dried thyme, and basil. Season with salt and pepper.
3. Spread the vegetable mixture in a baking dish and place it in the preheated oven.
4. Roast for 35-40 minutes, stirring occasionally, until vegetables are tender and slightly caramelized.

**For the Baked Polenta:**

1. As the vegetables roast, place a medium saucepan filled with water (or vegetable broth) and a small amount of salt to the boil.
2. Add the polenta gradually while whisking continuously to prevent lumps and lowering the heat to a low simmer.
3. Simmer, stirring regularly, for another 15 to 20 minutes, or until the polenta is cooked and the mixture thickens.
4. Take off the heat and, if you'd like, whisk in butter or olive oil for extra richness.
5. Transfer the polenta to a baking dish that has been coated with oil and level it out.
6. Bake in the oven (you can do this alongside the ratatouille) for about 20 minutes, or until the surface is firmer and slightly golden.

### Nutritional Information (per serving):

- Calories: 380 kcal • Protein: 8g • Carbohydrates: 60g • Fat: 14g • Saturated Fat: 2g (if using olive oil)
- Cholesterol: 0mg (if using olive oil) • Sodium: 280mg • Dietary Fiber: 11g • Sugars: 12g

## 6.2 Baked Lemon Chicken with Thyme

Servings: 2 | Preparation Time: 10 minutes | Cooking Time: 25-30 minutes

### INGREDIENTS:

- 2 boneless, skinless chicken breasts (about 1 pound or 450g)
- 2 tablespoons (30ml) olive oil
- 1 teaspoon (5g) garlic powder
- 1 teaspoon (5g) onion powder
- 1 teaspoon (2g) dried thyme
- Salt and black pepper, to taste
- Fresh lemon wedges for serving

### INSTRUCTIONS:

1. Preheat your oven to 400°F (200°C). Utilizing paper towels, pat dry the chicken breasts.
2. To make the seasoning, combine the olive oil, salt, black pepper, dried thyme, onion powder, and garlic powder in a small bowl.
3. Rub the seasoning mix evenly over both sides of the chicken breasts to coat them thoroughly.
4. After putting the spiced chicken in a baking dish, bake it in a preheated oven for 25 to 30 minutes, or until the internal temperature reaches 165°F (74°C).
5. Take it out of the oven and let it rest for a few minutes before slicing. Serve the chicken with fresh lemon wedges on the side.

### Nutritional Information (per serving):

• Calories: 295 kcal • Protein: 35g • Carbohydrates: 2g • Fat: 16g • Saturated Fat: 2g • Cholesterol: 94mg • Sodium: 200mg • Dietary Fiber: 0.5g • Sugars: 0g

## 6.3 Maple Glazed Salmon with Quinoa

Servings: 2 | Preparation Time: 10 minutes | Cooking Time: 20 minutes

### INGREDIENTS:

**For the Salmon:**

- 2 (6-ounce or 170g each) salmon fillets
- 1 tablespoon (15ml) pure maple syrup
- 1 teaspoon (5ml) Dijon mustard
- 1/2 teaspoon (2ml) soy sauce or tamari (for a gluten-free option)
- 1 clove garlic, minced
- Salt and freshly ground black pepper, to taste

**For the Quinoa:**

- 1/2 cup (90g) quinoa, rinsed
- 1 cup (240ml) water or vegetable broth
- Pinch of salt

### INSTRUCTIONS:

**For the Quinoa:**

1. Rinse the quinoa and add water (or veggie broth) and a teaspoon of salt to a small pot.
2. Over medium-high heat, bring to a boil; after that, lower the heat to a simmer and cover.
3. Simmer until the quinoa is soft and fluffy, about 15 minutes, or until all the liquid has been absorbed.
4. Take it off the heat and leave it covered for five minutes. Fluff with a fork before serving.

**For the Maple Glazed Salmon:**

1. Preheat your oven to 375°F (190°C).
2. Combine the soy sauce, maple syrup, minced garlic, and Dijon mustard in a small bowl.
3. To facilitate quick cleanup, lay the salmon fillets on a baking sheet covered with foil or parchment paper after seasoning them with salt and pepper.
4. Brush the maple mixture over the salmon fillets, coating them evenly.
5. Bake for 12 to 15 minutes, or until a fork can easily pierce the salmon, in a preheated oven.

**Nutritional Information (per serving):**

• Calories: 480 kcal • Protein: 39g • Carbohydrates: 39g • Fat: 18g • Saturated Fat: 3g • Cholesterol: 75mg
• Sodium: 230mg • Dietary Fiber: 4g • Sugars: 7g

## 6.4 Stuffed Portobello Mushrooms

**Servings: 2 | Preparation Time: 15 minutes**
**Cooking Time: 20 minutes**

### INGREDIENTS:

• 4 large portobello mushrooms, stems removed and gills scraped out
• 1 tablespoon (15ml) olive oil, plus extra for brushing
• 1/2 cup (75g) diced red bell peppers
• 1/2 cup (75g) diced onions
• 2 cloves garlic, minced
• 1/2 cup (90g) cooked quinoa or brown rice
• 1/4 cup (30g) feta cheese or a dairy-free alternative
• 1 tablespoon (15g) chopped fresh parsley
• Salt and freshly ground black pepper, to taste
• Optional: 1/4 cup (25g) breadcrumbs for topping (use gluten-free if necessary)

### INSTRUCTIONS:

1. Preheat the oven to 375°F (190°C). Spread parchment paper on a baking pan or give it a quick oil.
2. Apply a thin layer of olive oil on the inside and outside of the portobello mushroom caps, then sprinkle with salt and pepper. Put them on the baking sheet that has been prepared, cap side down.
3. In a skillet set over medium heat, preheat 1 tablespoon of olive oil. Saute the chopped onions and bell peppers for 3-5 minutes, or until they become tender.
4. Simmer the minced garlic in the skillet for a further minute, or until it becomes aromatic.
5. In a bowl, mix together the cooked quinoa or brown rice, the sautéed vegetables, feta cheese, and chopped parsley. To taste, add more pepper and salt to the mixture.
6. After filling the mushroom caps with the mixture, lightly press down to compact the filling.
7. Optional: Sprinkle breadcrumbs over the stuffed mushrooms for a crispy topping.
8. The mushrooms should be soft, and the topping should be golden brown after about 20 minutes of baking in a preheated oven.
9. Serve the stuffed portobello mushrooms warm, garnished with additional parsley if desired.

**Nutritional Information (per serving):**

• Calories: 265 kcal • Protein: 9g • Carbohydrates: 30g • Fat: 13g • Saturated Fat: 3g • Cholesterol: 15mg
• Sodium: 310mg • Dietary Fiber: 5g • Sugars: 9g

# 6.5 Lemon Herb Roasted Cod

Servings: 2 | Preparation Time: 10 minutes | Cooking Time: 15 minutes

## INGREDIENTS:

- 2 (6-ounce) cod fillets
- 1 tablespoon (15ml) olive oil
- 1 lemon, zest and juice divided
- 2 cloves garlic, minced
- 1 teaspoon (5ml) fresh thyme leaves
- 1 teaspoon (5ml) fresh parsley, chopped
- Salt and freshly ground black pepper, to taste

## INSTRUCTIONS:

1. Preheat the oven to 400°F (200°C).
2. After using paper towels to pat dry, put the cod fillets in a baking dish.
3. Olive oil, garlic, thyme, parsley, and half of the lemon juice should all be combined in a small bowl. Stir well to mix the herbs and garlic into the oil.
4. Spoon the herb mixture over the cod fillets, ensuring they are well coated. Add freshly ground black pepper and salt for seasoning.
5. Bake the fish for 12 to 15 minutes, or until it flakes easily with a fork, in a preheated oven.
6. Remove from the oven and drizzle the remaining lemon juice over the cooked fillets. Garnish with lemon zest for extra freshness and flavor.

## Nutritional Information (per serving):

• Calories: 195 kcal • Protein: 31g • Carbohydrates: 3g • Fat: 7g • Saturated Fat: 1g • Cholesterol: 60mg
• Sodium: 95mg • Dietary Fiber: 0.5g • Sugars: 0.6g

# Chapter 7: Global Favorites

## 7.1 Greek Chicken with Tzatziki Sauce

Servings: 2 | Preparation Time: 30 minutes | Cooking Time: 8 minutes

**INGREDIENTS:**

**For Chicken Skewers:**

- 2 boneless, skinless chicken breasts (about 12 oz or 340g total), cut into bite-sized cubes
- 2 tablespoons (30ml) olive oil
- 2 teaspoons dried oregano
- 2 teaspoons dried thyme
- 2 teaspoons smoked paprika
- 2 cloves garlic, minced
- Salt and black pepper, to taste
- Cherry tomatoes, for skewering
- Red onion, for skewering

**For Tzatziki:**

- 1/2 cup (120g) Greek yogurt
- 1/2 cucumber, finely diced
- 2 cloves garlic, minced
- 2 teaspoons fresh dill, chopped
- 2 teaspoons lemon juice
- Salt and black pepper, to taste

**INSTRUCTIONS:**

1. Begin by preparing the marinade. Mix olive oil, dried oregano, dried thyme, smoked paprika, minced garlic, salt, and black pepper in a bowl to create the marinade. Coat the chicken cubes completely by adding them to the marinade. Let them marinate for at least 15-30 minutes.

2. To make the tzatziki sauce, take another bowl and mix Greek yogurt, finely diced cucumber, minced garlic, chopped fresh dill, lemon juice, salt, and black pepper. Once fully combined, chill until ready to serve.

3. On medium-high heat, preheat a grill or grill pan.

4. Thread the marinated chicken cubes, cherry tomatoes, and red onion onto skewers, alternating the ingredients.

5. Grill the chicken skewers for about 3-4 minutes per side or until the chicken is cooked through and has grill marks. Ensure the chicken is no longer pink in the center and the juices run clear.

6. Serve the chicken skewers with the chilled tzatziki sauce on the side.

**Nutritional Information (per serving):**

• Calories: 1791 kcal • Protein: 95g • Carbohydrates: 20g • Fat: 148g • Saturated Fat: 17.5g

• Cholesterol: 267.5mg • Sodium: 707.5mg • Dietary Fiber: 4g • Sugars: 9g

# 7.2 Moroccan Vegetable Tagine with Couscous

Servings: 2 | Preparation Time: 20 minutes | Cooking Time: 40 minutes

## INGREDIENTS:

### For Vegetable Tagine:
- 1 small sweet potato, peeled and cubed
- 1 small zucchini, cubed
- 1 small yellow squash, cubed
- 1/2 bell pepper (any color), chopped
- 1/2 onion, chopped
- 2 cloves garlic, minced
- 1/2 cup (90g) chickpeas, cooked or canned
- 1/2 cup (100g) crushed tomatoes, canned or fresh
- 1/2 teaspoon ground cumin
- 1/2 teaspoon ground coriander
- 1/2 teaspoon ground cinnamon
- 1/4 teaspoon ground ginger
- 1/4 teaspoon paprika
- Pinch of cayenne pepper (optional)
- 2 cups (480ml) vegetable broth
- 2 tablespoons (30ml) olive oil
- Salt and black pepper, to taste
- Fresh cilantro, chopped, for garnish
- Toasted almonds, for garnish (optional)

### For the Couscous:
- 1 cup (180g) couscous (see "recall slice 1" for preparation instructions)
- 1 cup (240ml) vegetable broth or water
- Salt, to taste
- Fresh parsley, chopped, for garnish

## INSTRUCTIONS:

1. Heat the olive oil in a tagine pot or a deep skillet over medium heat. Add chopped onion and minced garlic and sauté until the onion is translucent.
2. Add the bell pepper, zucchini, sweet potato, and yellow squash and simmer for an additional 5 minutes.
3. Add the spices: ground cumin, coriander, cinnamon, ginger, paprika, and cayenne pepper. Stir to coat the vegetables.
4. Add the veggie broth and smashed tomatoes. After bringing it to a boil, lower the heat, cover it, and simmer the mixture until the veggies are soft for about 30 minutes.
5. After adding the cooked chickpeas, simmer for a further 10 minutes to let the flavors combine.

### Prepare the couscous:

1. The vegetable broth or water with a dash of salt should be brought to a boil in a small pot.
2. After adding the couscous, turn off the heat and cover. After five minutes, use a fork to fluff it up. Let it cool until it reaches room temperature.

### Nutritional Information (per serving):

- Calories: 560 kcal • Protein: 18g • Carbohydrates: 90g • Fat: 14g • Saturated Fat: 2g • Cholesterol: 0mg
- Sodium: 700mg • Dietary Fiber: 15g • Sugars: 12g

# 7.3 Cuban Black Beans and Rice

**Servings: 2 | Preparation Time: 10 minutes | Cooking Time: 25 minutes**

## INGREDIENTS:

### For Cuban Black Beans:

- 1 cup (200g) black beans, cooked or canned
- 1/2 onion, finely chopped
- 1 bell pepper, chopped (any color)
- 2 cloves garlic, minced
- 1/2 teaspoon ground cumin
- 1/2 teaspoon dried oregano
- 1 bay leaf
- 1 tablespoon (15ml) olive oil
- 1 tablespoon (15ml) apple cider vinegar
- 1/2 cup (120ml) vegetable broth or water
- Salt and black pepper, to taste
- Fresh cilantro, chopped, for garnish

### For the Rice:

- 1 cup (190g) long-grain white rice
- 2 cups (480ml) water
- 1/2 teaspoon salt

## INSTRUCTIONS:

1. Start by preparing the rice. Heat the water and salt in a medium pot until they boil. Add the rice, reduce heat to low, cover, and simmer for 18-20 minutes, until water is absorbed and rice is tender. Take it off the heat source and leave it covered for five minutes. Fluff with a fork before serving.

2. In another skillet, warm up some olive oil over medium heat while the rice cooks. Add the minced garlic, bell pepper, and onion, chopped. Simmer the veggies for 5 to 7 minutes, stirring them occasionally, or until they become tender.

3. Add the bay leaf, dried oregano, ground cumin, and cooked black beans and stir. Cook for an additional minute to allow the spices to become fragrant.

4. Add apple cider vinegar and vegetable broth or water. After bringing to a simmer, lower the heat and simmer for 15 minutes to let the flavors mingle. To taste, add salt and black pepper for seasoning. Discard the bay leaf before serving.

5. Serve the black beans over the prepared rice, garnished with fresh cilantro.

## Nutritional Information (per serving):

• Calories: 490 kcal • Protein: 16g • Carbohydrates: 87g • Fat: 7g • Saturated Fat: 1g • Cholesterol: 0mg
• Sodium: 300mg • Dietary Fiber: 13g • Sugars: 3g

# 7.4 Thai Green Curry with Tofu

Servings: 2 | Preparation Time: 15 minutes | Cooking Time: 25 minutes

## INGREDIENTS:

### For the Green Curry:

- 14 oz (400g) firm tofu, drained and pressed
- 1 tablespoon (15ml) vegetable oil
- 2 tablespoons green curry paste, adjust to taste
- 1/2 red bell pepper, sliced into thin strips
- 1/2 green bell pepper, sliced into thin strips
- 1/2 small zucchini, sliced
- 1/4 cup (50g) bamboo shoots, canned and drained
- 1 cup (240ml) coconut milk
- 1/2 cup (120ml) vegetable broth
- 1 tablespoon (15ml) soy sauce
- 1 teaspoon (5ml) brown sugar
- 1/2 tablespoon (7.5ml) lime juice
- Fresh basil leaves, for garnish

## INSTRUCTIONS:

1. Cut the tofu into bite-sized cubes.
2. In a big skillet or wok, warm the vegetable oil over medium heat. Stir the green curry paste in and heat, stirring constantly, for about 1 minute, until aromatic.
3. To the skillet, add the cut bell peppers and zucchini. The vegetables should start to soften after a few minutes of sautéing.
4. Add the veggie broth and coconut milk. Bring to a gentle simmer.
5. Gently add the tofu cubes and bamboo shoots to the curry. Stir carefully to combine without breaking the tofu.
6. Season with soy sauce and brown sugar. Simmer for about 15 minutes, allowing the tofu to absorb the flavors of the curry.
7. Take off the heat and mix in the lime juice. Adjust the seasoning if necessary.
8. Garnish with fresh basil leaves before serving. Serve the curry over cooked jasmine rice or with rice noodles, as preferred.

## Nutritional Information (per serving):

• Calories: 450 kcal • Protein: 22g • Carbohydrates: 20g • Fat: 32g • Saturated Fat: 20g • Cholesterol: 0mg
• Sodium: 650mg • Dietary Fiber: 3g • Sugars: 6g

# 7.5 Indian Lentil Dal with Spinach

Servings: 2 | Preparation Time: 10 minutes | Cooking Time: 35 minutes

## INGREDIENTS:

- 1 cup (200g) red lentils, rinsed
- 2 cups (480ml) vegetable broth
- 1/2 tablespoon (7.5ml) vegetable oil
- 1/2 onion, finely chopped
- 2 cloves garlic, minced
- 1 teaspoon (5ml) ginger, grated
- 1/2 teaspoon (2.5ml) ground turmeric
- 1/2 teaspoon (2.5ml) ground cumin
- 1/2 teaspoon (2.5ml) ground coriander
- 1/4 teaspoon (1.25ml) cayenne pepper (optional)
- 1 cup (120g) fresh spinach, roughly chopped
- Salt to taste
- 1/2 lemon, juiced
- Fresh cilantro, for garnish

## INSTRUCTIONS:

1. The vegetable broth should be brought to a boil in a big pot. Add the rinsed red lentils and simmer on low heat, partially covered, stirring occasionally to prevent sticking. Cook for about 20 minutes or until the lentils are tender.

2. In a pan over medium heat, warm the vegetable oil while the lentils are cooking. Add the chopped onion, minced garlic, and grated ginger. Cook for 5 to 7 minutes, or until the onion is aromatic and transparent.

3. Add the ground turmeric, ground cumin, ground coriander, and cayenne pepper to the onion mixture. Cook, stirring constantly, for another 2 minutes to allow the spices to release their flavors.

4. Once the lentils are tender, add the spiced onion mixture to the pot. Stir well to combine.

5. Add the chopped fresh spinach to the lentil dal, stirring until the spinach wilts and is fully incorporated about 3-5 minutes.

6. Toss in the lemon juice right before serving, and season with salt to taste.

7. Serve hot, garnished with fresh cilantro. Accompany with brown rice or whole-grain naan bread for a complete meal.

## Nutritional Information (per serving):

• Calories: 360 kcal • Protein: 22g • Carbohydrates: 60g • Fat: 5g • Saturated Fat: 0.5g • Cholesterol: 0mg

• Sodium: 300mg • Dietary Fiber: 15g • Sugars: 4g

# Chapter 8: Dinner Classics

## 8.1 Oven-Roasted Turkey Breast with Sweet Potatoes

Servings: 2 | Preparation Time: 15 minutes

Cooking Time: 1 hour

### INGREDIENTS:

- 1 turkey breast (about 1 lb or 450g), bone-in, skin-on
- 2 medium sweet potatoes, peeled and cut into 1-inch cubes
- 2 tablespoons (30ml) olive oil, divided
- 2 cloves garlic, minced
- 1 teaspoon (5ml) fresh thyme, chopped
- 1/2 teaspoon (2.5ml) fresh rosemary, chopped
- 1/2 teaspoon (2.5ml) fresh sage, chopped
- Salt and black pepper, to taste
- 1/2 cup (120ml) low-sodium chicken broth

### INSTRUCTIONS:

1. Preheat your oven to 375°F (190°C).
2. Place the sweet potatoes on a baking sheet, drizzle with 1 tablespoon (15ml) of olive oil, sprinkle with some salt and pepper, and toss to coat evenly. Roast for about 15 minutes, or until they begin to soften, in a preheated oven.
3. Meanwhile, mix 1 tablespoon (15ml) of olive oil with minced garlic, chopped thyme, rosemary, and sage in a small bowl.
4. Salt and black pepper are used to season the turkey breast. All over the turkey breast, rub the mixture of herbs and garlic.
5. Take the baking sheet out of the oven after the sweet potatoes have been roasting for 15 minutes.
6. Make space in the center and place the turkey breast on the baking sheet. Pour chicken broth over the turkey and sweet potatoes.
7. Return the baking sheet to the oven and continue to roast for about 45 minutes, or until an instant-read thermometer inserted into the thickest part of the breast registers 165°F (74°C).
8. Take the turkey out of the oven and give it 10 minutes to rest before slicing. Serve the cooked sweet potatoes alongside the turkey.

### Nutritional Information (per serving):

• Calories: 420 kcal • Protein: 55g • Carbohydrates: 28g • Fat: 10g • Saturated Fat: 2g • Cholesterol: 130mg

• Sodium: 250mg • Dietary Fiber: 4g • Sugars: 5g

# 8.2 Vegetarian Chili with Heart-Healthy Toppings

**Servings: 2 | Preparation Time: 20 minutes | Cooking Time: 40 minutes**

## INGREDIENTS:

### For the Chili:

- 1 tablespoon (15ml) olive oil
- 1 medium onion, diced
- 2 cloves garlic, minced
- 1 bell pepper (any color), diced
- 1 small zucchini, diced
- 1 carrot, peeled and diced
- 1 can (15 oz or 425g) diced tomatoes, with their juice
- 1 can (15 oz or 425g) kidney beans, drained and rinsed
- 1 can (15 oz or 425g) black beans, drained and rinsed
- 2 tablespoons (30ml) tomato paste
- 1 cup (240ml) vegetable broth
- 1 teaspoon (5ml) chili powder, or to taste
- 1/2 teaspoon (2.5ml) ground cumin
- Salt and pepper, to taste

### For the Heart-Healthy Toppings:

- 1 ripe avocado, peeled, pitted, and diced
- 1/2 cup (120g) plain Greek yogurt or dairy-free alternative
- Fresh cilantro, chopped
- Lime wedges, for serving

## INSTRUCTIONS:

1. In a big pot, warm the olive oil over medium heat. Add onion and sauté until translucent, about 5 minutes.
2. Add the minced garlic, diced bell pepper, zucchini, and carrot. Cook for another 5 minutes until the vegetables are softened.
3. Stir in diced tomatoes, kidney beans, black beans, tomato paste, vegetable broth, chili powder, and ground cumin. Season with salt and pepper.
4. Bring the mixture to a boil, then reduce the heat and let the chili simmer, covered, for about 30 minutes.
5. When required, add extra broth and stir occasionally until the desired consistency is achieved.
6. Once the chili is thickened and the vegetables are tender, adjust the seasoning to your preference.
7. When ready to serve, spoon the chili into bowls and garnish with chopped cilantro, cubed avocado, Greek yogurt, and lime juice.

## Nutritional Information (per serving):

• Calories: 450 kcal • Protein: 19g • Carbohydrates: 65g • Fat: 15g • Saturated Fat: 2g • Cholesterol: 5mg
• Sodium: 700mg • Dietary Fiber: 20g • Sugars: 12g

# 8.3 Slow Cooker Chicken Cacciatore

Servings: 2 | Preparation Time: 15 minutes | Cooking Time: 4 hours on high or 8 hours on low

## INGREDIENTS:

- 2 large chicken breasts, boneless and skinless (about 1 lb or 450g total)
- 1 can (15 oz or 425g) diced tomatoes
- 1/2 onion, sliced
- 1 bell pepper (any color), sliced
- 2 cloves garlic, minced
- 1/2 cup (120ml) low-sodium chicken broth
- 1 teaspoon (5ml) dried oregano
- 1/2 teaspoon (2.5ml) dried basil
- Salt and black pepper, to taste
- 1/2 cup (75g) sliced mushrooms
- 2 tablespoons (30ml) capers, drained
- 2 tablespoons (30ml) chopped fresh parsley, for garnish
- Cooked whole grain pasta or brown rice, for serving (optional)

## INSTRUCTIONS:

1. Black pepper and salt are used to season the chicken breasts. Place them at the bottom of the slow cooker.
2. Add the diced tomatoes (with juices), sliced onion, sliced bell pepper, minced garlic, chicken broth, dried oregano, and dried basil over the chicken.
3. To ensure the chicken is cooked through and tender, cook it covered for 4 hours on high or 8 hours on low.
4. About 30 minutes before the cooking time is up, add the sliced mushrooms and capers to the slow cooker. Stir gently to combine.
5. Once the chicken cacciatore is ready, adjust the seasoning to taste, and if desired, shred the chicken into large pieces using two forks.
6. Serve the chicken cacciatore garnished with chopped fresh parsley. Accompany with cooked whole grain pasta or brown rice for a complete meal.

## Nutritional Information (per serving, without pasta/rice):

• Calories: 290 kcal • Protein: 35g • Carbohydrates: 20g • Fat: 8g • Saturated Fat: 1.5g • Cholesterol: 90mg
• Sodium: 400mg • Dietary Fiber: 4g • Sugars: 10g

# 8.4 Vegan Mushroom Stroganoff

Servings: 2 | Preparation Time: 10 minutes | Cooking Time: 20 minutes

## INGREDIENTS:

- 2 cups (150g) mixed mushrooms (such as cremini, shiitake, and portobello), sliced
- 1 tablespoon (15ml) olive oil
- 1 small onion, finely chopped
- 2 cloves of garlic, minced
- 1/2 tablespoon (7.5ml) soy sauce (or tamari for a gluten-free option)
- 1 teaspoon (5ml) smoked paprika
- 2 tablespoons (30ml) all-purpose flour (gluten-free if necessary)
- 1 1/2 cups (360ml) vegetable broth
- 1/2 cup (120ml) unsweetened plant-based milk (such as almond, soy, or oat milk)
- Salt and black pepper, to taste
- Fresh parsley, chopped, for garnish

## INSTRUCTIONS:

1. Over medium heat, preheat the olive oil in a big pan. Add the onions and cook for about 3 minutes, or until they are transparent.
2. Add the minced garlic and cook for an additional minute once it becomes aromatic.
3. Increase the heat to medium-high, add the sliced mushrooms, and cook for 5-7 minutes until they have released their moisture and started to brown.
4. Add the smoked paprika and soy sauce, then simmer for an additional minute.
5. Once the flour has been added, thoroughly whisk the mixture of mushrooms to coat them.
6. Gradually add the vegetable broth while stirring continuously. Make sure there are no lumps of flour remaining.
7. Pour in the plant-based milk and lower the heat to a simmer. Stir continuously, and let it cook for another 5-10 minutes or until the sauce has thickened to your liking. To taste, add salt and black pepper for seasoning.
8. Once the stroganoff is thick and creamy, remove it from heat. Serve with your preferred mashed potatoes or noodles and sprinkle with fresh parsley.

Nutritional Information (per serving, without noodles/potatoes):

• Calories: 160 kcal • Protein: 6g • Carbohydrates: 18g • Fat: 8g • Saturated Fat: 1g • Cholesterol: 0mg
• Sodium: 600mg • Dietary Fiber: 3g • Sugars: 6g

# 8.5 Hearty Beef Stew

**Servings: 2 | Preparation Time: 20 minutes | Cooking Time: 2 hours**

## INGREDIENTS:

- 8 oz (225g) lean beef stew meat, trimmed of fat and cut into 1-inch pieces
- 1 tablespoon (15ml) olive oil
- 1 medium onion, chopped
- 2 cloves garlic, minced
- 2 medium carrots, peeled and chopped
- 2 celery stalks, chopped
- 1 small sweet potato, peeled and diced
- 1 can (15 oz or 425g) diced tomatoes, with their juice
- 2 cups (480ml) low-sodium beef broth
- 1 teaspoon (5ml) dried thyme
- 1 bay leaf
- Salt and freshly ground black pepper, to taste
- 1/2 cup (75g) frozen peas
- 2 teaspoons (10ml) cornstarch (optional, to thicken)
- 2 tablespoons (30ml) water (optional, to thicken)

## INSTRUCTIONS:

1. Add the olive oil to a big pot that has been preheated to medium-high heat. Brown the beef pieces on all sides for about 3-4 minutes. Remove beef and set aside.
2. Cook the chopped onion in the same saucepan for about 5 minutes, or until it becomes transparent. Cook for a further minute after adding the minced garlic.
3. Return the beef to the pot and add chopped carrots, celery, sweet potato, diced tomatoes with their juice, beef broth, dried thyme, and bay leaf. Season with salt and pepper.
4. After bringing the stew to a boil, turn down the heat. Cover and simmer for about 1 hour and 30 minutes, or until the beef is tender.
5. Cook for a further ten minutes after adding the frozen peas to the pot.
6. In a small bowl, make a slurry by mixing the cornstarch and water if you want the stew to be thicker. Once the appropriate thickness is reached, simmer the stew for an additional 5 minutes after stirring in the slurry.
7. Take off the bay leaf, taste, and adjust the seasoning.
8. Serve hot, perhaps with a side of crusty whole grain bread or over a bed of cooked quinoa for added fiber and nutrients.

## Nutritional Information (per serving):

• Calories: 380 kcal • Protein: 35g • Carbohydrates: 35g • Fat: 12g • Saturated Fat: 3g • Cholesterol: 70mg
• Sodium: 320mg • Dietary Fiber: 7g • Sugars: 12g

# Chapter 9: Sides and Small Plates

## 9.1 Zesty Quinoa Salad

**Servings: 2 | Preparation Time: 15 minutes | Cooking Time: 15 minutes**

## INGREDIENTS:

### For the Salad:

- 1/2 cup (90g) quinoa, rinsed
- 1 cup (240ml) water
- 1/2 cup (75g) cherry tomatoes, halved
- 1/2 cup (80g) canned black beans, drained and rinsed
- 1/4 cup (40g) corn kernels (fresh, canned, or frozen and thawed)
- 1/4 cup (40g) red bell pepper, diced
- 1/4 cup (30g) red onion, finely chopped
- 2 tablespoons (8g) fresh cilantro, chopped
- 1 avocado, diced
- Salt and pepper to taste

### For the Zesty Dressing:

- 3 tablespoons (45ml) extra virgin olive oil
- 2 tablespoons (30ml) fresh lime juice
- 1 teaspoon (5ml) red wine vinegar
- 1/2 teaspoon (2ml) honey (or agave syrup for a vegan option)
- 1/2 teaspoon cumin powder
- Salt and pepper to taste

## INSTRUCTIONS:

1. Cook the quinoa: In a medium saucepan, combine rinsed quinoa and water. After raising it to a boil, reduce heat to a simmer, cover it, and cook until water is completely absorbed, for about 15 minutes. Take off the heat and leave it covered for 5 minutes. Using a fork, fluff and let cool.

2. While the quinoa is cooling, in a large bowl, combine the cherry tomatoes, black beans, corn, red bell pepper, red onion, and cilantro.

3. Prepare the Zesty Dressing by whisking together the olive oil, lime juice, red wine vinegar, honey (or agave syrup), cumin powder, and salt and pepper in a small bowl.

4. Pour the Zesty Dressing over the salad after adding the cooled quinoa to the bowl with the veggies. Toss to combine all ingredients.

5. Make sure not to squash the diced avocado as you gently fold it in.

6. If necessary, add more salt and pepper to taste and adjust the seasoning.

7. Serve the Zesty Quinoa Salad chilled or at room temperature.

### Nutritional Information (per serving):

• Calories: 375 kcal • Protein: 9g • Carbohydrates: 45g • Fat: 20g • Saturated Fat: 2.5g • Cholesterol: 0mg
• Sodium: 15mg • Dietary Fiber: 11g • Sugars: 5g

## 9.2 Cauliflower Steaks with Herb Sauce

Servings: 2 | Preparation Time: 15 minutes | Cooking Time: 25 minutes

**INGREDIENTS:**

- 1 large head of cauliflower
- 2 tablespoons (30ml) olive oil, divided
- Salt and freshly ground black pepper, to taste

**For the Herb Sauce:**

- 1/2 cup (120ml) fresh parsley, finely chopped
- 1/4 cup (60ml) fresh cilantro, finely chopped
- 2 tablespoons (30ml) chives, finely chopped
- 1 clove garlic, minced
- 3 tablespoons (45ml) olive oil
- 1 tablespoon (15ml) apple cider vinegar
- 1 teaspoon (5ml) honey (or agave syrup for a vegan option)
- Salt and pepper, to taste

**INSTRUCTIONS:**

1. Preheat the oven to 400°F (200°C).
2. Remove the leaves from the cauliflower and cut the head into two 1-inch-thick slices or "steaks," retaining as much of the stem as possible to hold the steaks together.
3. Add salt and pepper to the cauliflower steaks after brushing them with 1 tablespoon of olive oil on each side.
4. After putting the cauliflower steaks on a parchment paper-lined baking sheet, preheat the oven and roast for 20 to 25 minutes, or until they are soft and golden brown.
5. Make the herb sauce in a basin with parsley, cilantro, chives, minced garlic, olive oil, apple cider vinegar, and honey (or agave syrup) while the cauliflower is roasting. Whisk until well combined and season with salt and pepper to taste.
6. Once the cauliflower is cooked, serve immediately with the herb sauce drizzled over the top.

**Nutritional Information (per serving):** • Calories: 295 kcal • Protein: 5g • Carbohydrates: 18g • Fat: 24g • Saturated Fat: 3.5g • Cholesterol: 0mg • Sodium: 89mg • Dietary Fiber: 7g • Sugars: 8g

## 9.3 Lemon Garlic Roasted Broccoli

Servings: 2 | Preparation Time: 10 minutes | Cooking Time: 20 minutes

**INGREDIENTS:**

- 1 large head of broccoli, cut into florets (about 1 pound or 450g)
- 2 tablespoons (30ml) olive oil
- 2 cloves garlic, minced
- Zest of 1 lemon
- 2 tablespoons (30ml) fresh lemon juice
- Salt and freshly ground black pepper, to taste

**INSTRUCTIONS:**

1. Preheat the oven to 425°F (220°C).
2. Toss the broccoli florets in a big basin with the lemon zest, olive oil, and minced garlic until well coated.
3. Spread the broccoli in a single layer on a baking sheet lined with parchment paper. Season with salt and black pepper.

4.  Bake the broccoli for 15 to 20 minutes, or until it's soft and the edges are crispy to your taste.
5.  When ready to serve, take the broccoli out of the oven and quickly sprinkle it with freshly squeezed lemon juice.

**Nutritional Information (per serving):**

• Calories: 154 kcal • Protein: 5g • Carbohydrates: 14g • Fat: 10g • Saturated Fat: 1.4g • Cholesterol: 0mg
• Sodium: 41mg • Dietary Fiber: 5g • Sugars: 3g

## 9.4 Balsamic Glazed Brussels Sprouts

**Servings: 2 | Preparation Time: 10 minutes**
**Cooking Time: 25 minutes**

**INGREDIENTS:**

•   2 cups (300g) Brussels sprouts, trimmed and halved
•   1 tablespoon (15ml) olive oil
•   Salt and freshly ground black pepper, to taste
•   2 tablespoons (30ml) balsamic vinegar
•   1 teaspoon (5ml) honey (or maple syrup for a vegan option)
•   Optional: Toasted almond slivers or chopped walnuts for garnish

**INSTRUCTIONS:**

1.  Preheat the oven to 400°F (200°C).
2.  Brussels sprouts cut in half should be evenly coated after tossing them in a mixture of olive oil, salt, and pepper. In a single layer, spread them out on a baking sheet covered with parchment paper.
3.  Stir the Brussels sprouts midway through to ensure equal roasting, and roast for about 20 minutes, or until they are tender and the edges have browned.
4.  As the Brussels sprouts roast, make the balsamic glaze in a small saucepan by combining the balsamic vinegar and honey (or maple syrup). Bring to a simmer over medium heat and reduce until slightly thickened, about 5 minutes.
5.  After roasting, take the Brussels sprouts out of the oven and toss them to coat well before drizzling them with the balsamic glaze.
6.  For extra texture and good fats, you can sprinkle chopped walnuts or slivered almonds on top.
7.  Serve warm as an inviting and flavorful side dish.

**Nutritional Information (per serving):**

• Calories: 130 kcal • Protein: 4g • Carbohydrates: 15g • Fat: 7g • Saturated Fat: 1g • Cholesterol: 0mg
• Sodium: 32mg • Dietary Fiber: 4g • Sugars: 7g

# 9.5 Sautéed Spinach with Pine Nuts and Raisins

**Servings: 2 | Preparation Time: 5 minutes**
**Cooking Time: 10 minutes**

## INGREDIENTS:

- 4 cups (120g) fresh spinach leaves, washed and stems removed
- 2 tablespoons (10g) pine nuts
- 1 tablespoon (15g) raisins
- 1 tablespoon (15ml) olive oil
- 1 garlic clove, minced
- Salt and freshly ground black pepper to taste
- A squeeze of fresh lemon juice (optional)

## INSTRUCTIONS:

1. To plump up the raisins, soak them in warm water for approximately 5 minutes in a small bowl and then drain.

2. Heat a large sauté pan or skillet over medium heat. After adding the pine nuts, roast them for 2-3 minutes, or until fragrant and golden brown. Be careful not to burn them. After the pine nuts are toasted, move them to another plate.

3. In the same pan, increase the heat to medium-high and add the olive oil and minced garlic. Sauté for about 1 minute until the garlic is fragrant but not browned.

4. Add the drained raisins and spinach to the pan. Season with salt and pepper and sauté for 2-3 minutes, or until the spinach has wilted.

5. Take off the heat, sprinkle in the toasted pine nuts, and mix everything together. If desired, drizzle a little lemon juice on top for an additional flavor boost.

6. Serve immediately as a warm and comforting side dish, rich in iron and packed with flavor.

**Nutritional Information (per serving):**

• Calories: 150 kcal • Protein: 3g • Carbohydrates: 10g • Fat: 11g • Saturated Fat: 1.5g • Cholesterol: 0mg
• Sodium: 97mg • Dietary Fiber: 3g • Sugars: 5g

# Chapter 10: Whole Grain Goodness

## 10.1 Whole Wheat Pasta Primavera

**Servings: 2 | Preparation Time: 10 minutes | Cooking Time: 20 minutes**

### INGREDIENTS:

- 4 oz (112g) whole wheat spaghetti or pasta of your choice
- 1 tablespoon (15ml) olive oil
- 1/2 onion, finely chopped
- 1 clove garlic, minced
- 1/2 bell pepper, diced
- 1/2 zucchini, diced
- 1/2 carrot, grated
- 1/2 can (7 oz / 200g) diced tomatoes
- 1/2 can (3 oz / 85g) tomato paste
- 1/2 teaspoon dried basil
- 1/2 teaspoon dried oregano
- Salt and pepper to taste
- Fresh basil leaves, for garnish (optional)
- Grated Parmesan cheese or nutritional yeast, for serving (optional)

### INSTRUCTIONS:

1. Cook the whole wheat spaghetti or pasta to al dente according to the package directions. Drain and set aside.
2. In a large skillet set over medium heat, warm the olive oil while the pasta cooks.
3. In the oil, sauté the onion and garlic for about 2 minutes, or until the onion becomes transparent.
4. Add the bell pepper, zucchini, and grated carrot to the skillet. Sauté the vegetables for 5 to 7 minutes, stirring periodically, or until they are soft.
5. Incorporate the tomato paste and diced tomatoes. Season the vegetable mixture with dried basil, oregano, salt, and pepper. To let the flavors combine, simmer for a further 5 minutes.
6. Toss the cooked whole wheat pasta with the vegetable sauce until evenly coated.
7. Garnish the spaghetti primavera with freshly chopped basil leaves and, if preferred, some grated Parmesan cheese or nutritional yeast.

### Nutritional Information (per serving):

- Calories: 315 kcal • Protein: 10g • Carbohydrates: 55g • Fat: 8g • Saturated Fat: 1g • Cholesterol: 0mg
- Sodium: 210mg • Dietary Fiber: 10g • Sugars: 10g

# 10.2 Barley and Mushroom Pilaf

Servings: 2 | Preparation Time: 10 minutes | Cooking Time: 40 minutes

## INGREDIENTS:

- 1/2 cup (100g) pearl barley, rinsed
- 2 cups (480ml) low-sodium vegetable broth
- 1 tablespoon (15ml) olive oil
- 1/2 onion, chopped
- 2 cloves garlic, minced
- 1 cup (100g) mushrooms, sliced
- 1/4 cup (60ml) white wine (optional)
- 1/2 teaspoon dried thyme
- Salt and pepper to taste
- Fresh parsley, chopped for garnish

## INSTRUCTIONS:

1. In a medium saucepan, bring the vegetable broth to a boil. After adding the washed barley, turn down the heat. Cover and simmer for about 30-40 minutes, or until the barley is tender and the liquid has been absorbed.
2. In a large skillet over medium heat, warm the olive oil while the barley cooks.
3. When the garlic and onion are added, sauté them for 2-3 minutes, or until the garlic is fragrant and the onion is transparent.
4. After adding the mushrooms to the skillet, sauté them for 5-7 minutes, or until they are browned and have shed their moisture.
5. If using white wine, pour it into the skillet now and allow it to cook off for a few minutes.
6. Add the dried thyme and adjust the seasoning with salt and pepper to taste.
7. Once the barley is cooked, if there's any excess liquid, drain it off. Then add the barley to the skillet with the mushrooms and onions.
8. Cook for a further 2-3 minutes to allow the flavors to meld after thoroughly stirring to incorporate all of the ingredients.
9. Check for seasoning and adjust if necessary. Remove from heat.
10. Serve the barley and mushroom pilaf garnished with chopped fresh parsley for a fresh, herby finish.

## Nutritional Information (per serving):

• Calories: 310 kcal • Protein: 8g • Carbohydrates: 55g • Fat: 7g • Saturated Fat: 1g • Cholesterol: 0mg

• Sodium: 120mg • Dietary Fiber: 10g • Sugars: 3g

# 10.3 Buckwheat Noodle Bowl

Servings: 2 | Preparation Time: 10 minutes | Cooking Time: 10 minutes

## INGREDIENTS:

- 4 oz (112g) buckwheat soba noodles
- 2 cups (475ml) low-sodium vegetable broth
- 1 cup (100g) shredded cabbage
- 1 medium carrot, julienned
- 1/2 red bell pepper, thinly sliced
- 1/2 cup (75g) shelled edamame, cooked
- 2 green onions, thinly sliced
- 1 tablespoon (15ml) low-sodium soy sauce
- 1 tablespoon (15ml) rice vinegar
- 1 teaspoon (5ml) sesame oil
- 1 teaspoon (5g) grated fresh ginger
- Optional: sesame seeds, for garnish

## INSTRUCTIONS:

1. Boil the soba noodles in water for 4–5 minutes, or as directed on the package.
2. Drain and rinse under cold water to prevent sticking. Set aside.
3. Simmer the vegetable stock gently in a medium-sized pot.
4. Cook the red bell pepper, carrot, and cabbage in the broth for 2-3 minutes, or until they are crisp but still slightly soft.
5. Stir in the cooked edamame, allowing it to warm through in the broth.
6. Mix the sesame oil, rice vinegar, soy sauce, and grated ginger in a small bowl to make a dressing.
7. Divide the cooked soba noodles between two bowls.
8. Ladle the simmering vegetable and broth mixture over the noodles in each bowl.
9. Drizzle the prepared dressing over the top of each noodle bowl.
10. If preferred, garnish with sesame seeds and sliced green onions.

## Nutritional Information (per serving):

• Calories: 320 kcal • Protein: 14g • Carbohydrates: 55g • Fat: 7g • Saturated Fat: 1g • Cholesterol: 0mg

• Sodium: 300mg • Dietary Fiber: 5g • Sugars: 5g

# 10.4 Oat and Banana Nut Waffles

Servings: 2 | Preparation Time: 10 minutes | Cooking Time: 10 minutes

## INGREDIENTS:

- 1 cup (90g) rolled oats
- 2 ripe bananas
- 2 large eggs
- 1/2 cup (120ml) milk (any type you prefer)
- 1/4 cup (30g) chopped nuts (such as walnuts or almonds)
- 1 teaspoon baking powder
- 1/2 teaspoon vanilla extract
- Pinch of salt
- Butter or cooking spray for the waffle iron

## INSTRUCTIONS:

1. Combine the rolled oats, ripe bananas, eggs, milk, chopped nuts, vanilla extract, baking powder, and a pinch of salt in a blender.
2. Blend the components until a smooth and well-combined mixture is achieved.
3. Allow the batter to rest for approximately 5-10 minutes. This helps the oats absorb the liquid and gives you fluffier waffles.
4. Heat your waffle iron according to the manufacturer's instructions. Once heated, apply a small amount of butter or cooking spray to coat the surface to prevent sticking.
5. Transfer half of the batter to the waffle iron's center. The waffle should be cooked until crisp and golden, so cover and cook. This should take about 5 minutes, but follow your waffle iron's indicator or check manually.
6. Carefully remove the cooked waffle and repeat with the remaining batter for the second serving.
7. Warm oat and banana nut waffles can be served warm with a dollop of yogurt, fresh fruit, or honey drizzled over.

## Nutritional Information (per serving):

• Calories: 290 kcal • Protein: 12g • Carbohydrates: 38g • Fat: 11g • Saturated Fat: 2g • Cholesterol: 186mg
• Sodium: 250mg • Dietary Fiber: 5g • Sugars: 10g

# 10.5 Wild Rice and Herb Salad

**Servings: 2 | Preparation Time: 15 minutes | Cooking Time: 45-50 minutes**

## INGREDIENTS:

- 1/2 cup (100g) wild rice
- 2 cups (480ml) water or low-sodium vegetable broth
- 1/2 cup (75g) cherry tomatoes, halved
- 1/4 cup (40g) diced cucumber
- 1/4 cup (30g) diced red onion
- 1/4 cup (15g) chopped fresh parsley
- 2 tablespoons (10g) chopped fresh dill
- 1 tablespoon (15ml) extra-virgin olive oil
- 1 tablespoon (15ml) fresh lemon juice
- Salt and pepper to taste
- Optional: 1 tablespoon (9g) toasted pine nuts for garnish

## INSTRUCTIONS:

1. Boil 2 cups of water or low-sodium vegetable broth in a medium saucepan. After adding the wild rice, lower the heat to a simmer. For 45 to 50 minutes, or until the rice is soft and the kernels start to pop, simmer the rice covered.
2. After cooking, remove any remaining liquid from the rice and let it cool somewhat.
3. In a large bowl, combine the cooled wild rice, halved cherry tomatoes, diced cucumber, diced red onion, chopped parsley, and fresh dill.
4. In a small bowl, whisk together the extra-virgin olive oil, fresh lemon juice, salt, and pepper to create a simple dressing.
5. After pouring the dressing over the salad, mix everything to ensure that the components are uniformly coated.
6. Taste and adjust the seasoning if needed. To enable the flavors to combine, let the salad rest for a few minutes.
7. Serve the wild rice and herb salad topped with toasted pine nuts if desired for added texture and flavor.

### Nutritional Information (per serving):

• Calories: 240 kcal • Protein: 6g • Carbohydrates: 40g • Fat: 7g • Saturated Fat: 1g • Cholesterol: 0mg
• Sodium: 10mg • Dietary Fiber: 4g • Sugars: 3g

# Chapter 11: Plant-Based Delights

## 11.1 Lentil Bolognese with Zucchini Noodles

Servings: 2 | Preparation Time: 15 minutes | Cooking Time: 30 minutes

### INGREDIENTS:

- 1/2 cup (100g) dry green lentils
- 2 large zucchinis
- 1 tablespoon (15ml) olive oil
- 1/2 onion, finely chopped
- 2 cloves garlic, minced
- 1 carrot, diced
- 1 celery stalk, diced
- 1 can (14oz/400g) diced tomatoes
- 1 tablespoon (15ml) tomato paste
- 1/2 teaspoon dried oregano
- 1/2 teaspoon dried basil
- Salt and pepper to taste
- Fresh basil leaves, for garnish (optional)
- Nutritional yeast or vegan Parmesan cheese, for serving (optional)

### INSTRUCTIONS:

1. After rinsing, simmer the lentils as directed on the package for 20 to 25 minutes, or until they are soft but not mushy. Drain any excess water and set aside.
2. While the lentils are cooking, use a spiralizer to turn the zucchinis into noodles. Set your zucchini noodles (also known as zoodles) aside.
3. Over medium heat, preheat the olive oil in a big pan. Saute the onion and garlic for around 5 minutes, or until the onion becomes transparent.
4. After adding the chopped celery and carrot to the skillet, sauté them for a further 5 minutes, or until they start to get tender.
5. Add the cooked lentils, dry oregano, dried basil, chopped tomatoes (with their liquid), and tomato paste. After bringing the mixture to a simmer and lowering the heat, cook it for about 10 minutes without covering. The sauce should thicken slightly. Season with salt and pepper to taste.
6. Just before the sauce is ready, steam the zucchini noodles for about 2-3 minutes until they are just tender. Be careful not to overcook them, or they will become mushy.
7. To serve, divide the zucchini noodles between two plates and top with the lentil bolognese sauce. If desired, garnish with vegan Parmesan cheese or nutritional yeast and fresh basil leaves.

### Nutritional Information (per serving):

• Calories: 330 kcal • Protein: 18g • Carbohydrates: 51g • Fat: 7g • Saturated Fat: 1g • Cholesterol: 0mg

• Sodium: 250mg • Dietary Fiber: 16g • Sugars: 12g

# 11.2 Stuffed Acorn Squash with Wild Rice

**Servings: 2 | Preparation Time: 15 minutes | Cooking Time: 60 minutes**

## INGREDIENTS:

- 1 acorn squash, halved and seeds removed
- 1/2 cup (100g) wild rice
- 1 1/4 cups (300ml) vegetable broth or water
- 1 tablespoon olive oil
- 1/4 cup (40g) diced onion
- 1 clove garlic, minced
- 1/4 cup (30g) diced bell pepper
- 1/4 cup (30g) diced carrots
- 1/4 cup (15g) dried cranberries
- 1/4 cup (15g) chopped pecans or walnuts (optional)
- Salt and pepper to taste
- A pinch of dried thyme
- Fresh parsley for garnish

## INSTRUCTIONS:

1. Preheat the oven to 375°F (190°C). Place the acorn squash halves cut-side down on a baking sheet lined with parchment paper and roast until fork-tender, about 40-45 minutes.
2. Make the wild rice as the squash roasts. The vegetable broth should be brought to a boil in a saucepan. After adding the wild rice, lower the heat to a simmer, cover, and let the rice cook for about 45 minutes, or until it is soft and has absorbed the liquid.
3. Over medium heat, preheat the olive oil in a skillet. Sauté the diced onion and garlic until translucent, about 3-4 minutes. After adding the carrots and bell pepper, sauté for a further 5 minutes.
4. Stir the cooked wild rice, dried cranberries, nuts (if using), salt, pepper, and dried thyme into the vegetable mixture until well combined.
5. Turn the roasted acorn squash halves cut-side up and divide the wild rice stuffing between them, packing it lightly.
6. Place the stuffed squash back in the oven and bake it for a further 15 to 20 minutes, or until the stuffing is thoroughly cooked.
7. Garnish with fresh parsley before serving.

## Nutritional Information (per serving):

• Calories: 315 kcal • Protein: 6g • Carbohydrates: 53g • Fat: 9g • Saturated Fat: 1g • Cholesterol: 0mg

• Sodium: 320mg • Dietary Fiber: 8g • Sugars: 12g

# 11.3 Vegan Tacos with Quinoa and Black Beans

Servings: 2 | Preparation Time: 20 minutes | Cooking Time: 25 minutes

## INGREDIENTS:

- 4 small corn tortillas
- 1/2 cup (90g) quinoa, rinsed
- 1 cup (240ml) vegetable broth or water
- 1 can (15 oz / 425g) black beans, drained and rinsed
- 1 tablespoon (15ml) olive oil
- 1/4 cup (40g) diced red onion
- 1 clove garlic, minced
- 1/2 teaspoon ground cumin
- 1/2 teaspoon paprika
- 1/2 teaspoon chili powder
- Salt and pepper to taste
- 1/4 cup (60g) fresh salsa
- 1 avocado, diced
- 1/4 cup (15g) chopped fresh cilantro
- Lime wedges for serving

## INSTRUCTIONS:

1. Place the washed quinoa and vegetable broth in a saucepan. After bringing to a boil, lower the heat to low, cover the pot, and simmer the quinoa for 15 minutes or until it becomes fluffy and the liquid has been absorbed. Take it off the stove, give it five minutes to rest, and then fluff it with a fork.

2. As the quinoa cooks, warm up some olive oil in a skillet over medium heat. Add the red onion and garlic, and sauté until soft and fragrant, for about 3 minutes.

3. Add the black beans to the skillet with the onion and garlic. Stir in the ground cumin, paprika, chili powder, salt, and pepper. Cook for a few minutes until the beans are heated through.

4. To make the corn tortillas malleable, reheat them in the microwave or on a dry skillet.

5. To assemble the tacos, lay the warmed tortillas flat and divide the quinoa evenly among them, followed by the black bean mixture.

6. Top each taco with fresh salsa, diced avocado, and chopped cilantro.

7. Lime wedges are served beside the tacos so that they can be squeezed over the top.

## Nutritional Information (per serving):

• Calories: 370 kcal • Protein: 12g • Carbohydrates: 50g • Fat: 15g • Saturated Fat: 2g • Cholesterol: 0mg

• Sodium: 530mg • Dietary Fiber: 12g • Sugars: 3g

# 11.4 Hearty Vegetable Pot Pie

Servings: 2 | Preparation Time: 30 minutes | Cooking Time: 35 minutes

## INGREDIENTS:

- 1 tablespoon (15ml) olive oil
- 1/2 onion, diced
- 1 carrot, diced
- 1 celery stalk, diced
- 1/4 cup (40g) frozen peas
- 1/4 cup (40g) frozen corn
- 1 small potato, peeled and diced
- 1/4 teaspoon dried thyme
- 1/4 teaspoon dried rosemary
- Salt and pepper to taste
- 1 1/2 tablespoons (15g) all-purpose flour or whole wheat flour
- 1 cup (240ml) vegetable broth
- 1/4 cup (60ml) unsweetened almond milk or any plant-based milk
- 1 sheet of puff pastry or pie crust, thawed if frozen (choose a vegan brand if necessary)
- 1 small beaten egg or plant-based milk for brushing the crust (optional)

## INSTRUCTIONS:

1. Preheat the oven to 400°F (200°C).
2. Place the olive oil in a big skillet and heat it to medium. Sauté the onion, carrot, and celery until they start to soften, about 5 minutes.
3. Add the frozen peas, corn, and diced potato, along with the dried thyme, rosemary, salt, and pepper. Cook for another 5 minutes.
4. To get rid of the taste of raw flour, sprinkle flour over the vegetables, stir, and simmer for one minute.
5. Add the almond milk and vegetable broth to the skillet gradually, stirring frequently for 3 to 4 minutes, or until the mixture thickens into a sauce. Once thickened, remove from heat.
6. Pour the vegetable filling into two small pie dishes or one larger dish.
7. On a surface dusted with flour just a bit, roll out the pie crust or puff pastry. Cut the dough to fit the top of the pie dishes. Place the dough over the filling and trim any excess. Using a fork to press, seal the edges. Make a few incisions on top to let out the steam.
8. Brush the top of the pie with a beaten egg or plant-based milk for a golden finish.
9. Bake for 35 to 40 minutes in a preheated oven, or until the filling is bubbling and the crust is golden brown.
10. Before serving, let the pot pie cool for a few minutes.

### Nutritional Information (per serving):

- Calories: 560 kcal • Protein: 10g • Carbohydrates: 65g • Sodium: 650mg • Dietary Fiber: 7g • Sugars: 5g
- Fat: 30g (Note: This can vary with the type of crust used)
- Saturated Fat: 7g (Note: This can vary with the type of crust used)
- Cholesterol: 10mg (If using an egg for the crust; otherwise 0mg)

# 11.5 Tempeh Stir Fry with Broccoli

Servings: 2 | Preparation Time: 10 minutes | Cooking Time: 20 minutes

## INGREDIENTS:

- 8 oz (225g) tempeh, cut into 1/2-inch cubes
- 2 cups (approx. 150g) broccoli florets
- 1 tablespoon (15ml) sesame oil or any vegetable oil
- 2 cloves garlic, minced
- 1 teaspoon fresh ginger, grated
- 1 small red bell pepper, thinly sliced
- 2 tablespoons soy sauce (or tamari for a gluten-free option)
- 1 tablespoon (15ml) maple syrup or agave nectar
- 1 teaspoon (5ml) rice vinegar
- 1/2 teaspoon cornstarch or arrowroot powder
- 1 tablespoon (15ml) water
- Sesame seeds for garnish
- Cooked brown rice or quinoa for serving

## INSTRUCTIONS:

1. After 3–4 minutes of steaming, the broccoli florets should be bright green and somewhat soft. Set aside.
2. In a big wok or skillet, warm the sesame oil over medium-high heat. Add the tempeh cubes and stir-fry until they are golden brown on all sides, about 5 minutes. After taking the tempeh out of the skillet, set it aside.
3. Add a little additional oil to the same skillet if necessary, and sauté the red bell pepper, grated ginger, and minced garlic for 2-3 minutes, or until the vegetables begin to soften.
4. Mix the soy sauce, water, rice vinegar, maple syrup, and cornstarch in a small basin. Pour this sauce into the skillet with the vegetables and cook for about 1 minute until the sauce begins to thicken.
5. Return the tempeh to the skillet, add the steamed broccoli, and toss everything together until the tempeh and broccoli are well coated with the sauce and heated through.
6. Top the cooked brown rice or quinoa with the tempeh stir-fry, and top with sesame seeds.

## Nutritional Information (per serving):

• Calories: 350 kcal • Protein: 21g • Carbohydrates: 27g • Fat: 20g • Saturated Fat: 3g • Cholesterol: 0mg
• Sodium: 720mg • Dietary Fiber: 5g • Sugars: 9g

# Chapter 12: Seafood Specialties

## 12.1 Grilled Shrimp with Avocado Salad

**Servings: 2 | Preparation Time: 15 minutes | Cooking Time: 10 minutes**

### INGREDIENTS:

- 12 large shrimp, peeled and deveined
- 1 tablespoon (15ml) olive oil
- 1 teaspoon (5ml) lime juice
- 1/2 teaspoon chili powder
- 1/2 teaspoon garlic powder
- Salt and pepper to taste
- 1 ripe avocado, diced
- 1 cup (about 150g) cherry tomatoes, halved
- 1/4 red onion, thinly sliced
- 2 cups (40g) mixed salad greens or lettuce of choice
- 2 tablespoons (30ml) extra virgin olive oil
- 1 tablespoon (15ml) balsamic vinegar
- Additional lime wedges for serving

### INSTRUCTIONS:

1. Preheat your grill to medium-high heat.
2. Add the shrimp, lime juice, chili powder, garlic powder, a small amount of salt, and pepper to a bowl and stir. Make sure the shrimp are well coated with the marinade.
3. Thread the shrimp onto skewers (soak wooden skewers in water for at least 20 minutes beforehand to prevent burning).
4. Grill the shrimp on the preheated grill for 2-3 minutes per side, or until they turn pink and are cooked through. Be careful not to overcook them.
5. For the avocado salad, combine the diced avocado, cherry tomatoes, and red onion in a large bowl. Gently stir to mix the ingredients without mashing the avocado.
6. In a small bowl, whisk together the extra virgin olive oil and balsamic vinegar to create a dressing. Drizzle this over the avocado salad and toss lightly to coat.
7. Divide the mixed salad greens between two plates. Top each with half of the avocado salad.
8. Once the shrimp are cooked, remove them from the skewers and divide them evenly atop the salad on each plate.
9. Serve with additional lime wedges to squeeze over the shrimp and salad as desired.

### Nutritional Information (per serving):

• Calories: 400 kcal • Protein: 24g • Carbohydrates: 14g • Fat: 29g • Saturated Fat: 4g • Cholesterol: 180mg
• Sodium: 300mg • Dietary Fiber: 7g • Sugars: 4g

## 12.2 Seared Scallops with Citrus Quinoa

Servings: 2 | Preparation Time: 10 minutes | Cooking Time: 20 minutes

### INGREDIENTS:

- 10 large sea scallops
- 1 tablespoon (15ml) olive oil
- Salt and pepper to taste
- 1/2 cup (95g) quinoa, rinsed
- 1 cup (240ml) water or vegetable broth
- Zest and juice of 1 orange
- Zest and juice of 1 lemon
- 1 tablespoon (15ml) extra virgin olive oil
- 1/4 cup (15g) chopped fresh parsley
- 1/2 avocado, diced
- A handful of toasted almond slices for garnish (optional)

### INSTRUCTIONS:

1. Cook the quinoa by combining the rinsed quinoa with water or vegetable broth in a small saucepan. Bring to a boil, then reduce heat to a low simmer, cover, and let it cook until all the liquid is absorbed and the quinoa is fluffy, about 15 minutes.
2. Once the quinoa is done, fluff it with a fork and stir in the orange and lemon zest, citrus juices, extra virgin olive oil, and chopped parsley. Gently fold in the diced avocado and set aside to let the flavors meld.
3. After using a paper towel to pat the scallops dry, season them on both sides with salt and pepper.
4. One tablespoon of olive oil should be heated in a nonstick skillet or cast-iron pan over medium-high heat.
5. Place the seasoned scallops in the pan without overcrowding. Sear for about 1 1/2 to 2 minutes on each side, or until they develop a golden crust and are just cooked through (they should feel slightly firm to the touch). Be careful not to overcook as they can become tough.
6. Divide the citrus quinoa between two plates. Top with the seared scallops and garnish with toasted almond slices if desired.

Nutritional Information (per serving): • Calories: 380 kcal • Protein: 23g • Carbohydrates: 33g

• Fat: 18g (including the healthy fats from avocado and olive oil) • Saturated Fat: 2g • Cholesterol: 37mg

• Sodium: 500mg (can vary based on the salt used in seasoning and the broth)

• Dietary Fiber: 5g • Sugars: 3g (natural sugars from the orange and lemon)

## 12.3 Pan-Seared Salmon with Mango Salsa

Servings: 2 | Preparation Time: 15 minutes | Cooking Time: 10 minutes

### INGREDIENTS:

- 2 salmon fillets (about 6 oz or 170g each), skin on
- 1 tablespoon (15ml) olive oil
- Salt and pepper to taste
- 1 ripe mango, peeled and diced
- 1/4 red onion, finely chopped
- 1/2 jalapeño, deseeded and minced (adjust to taste)
- Juice of 1 lime
- 1/4 cup (10g) fresh cilantro, chopped
- 1 small avocado, diced

## INSTRUCTIONS:

1. Salt and pepper should be used to season the salmon fillets on both sides.
2. Heat the olive oil in a non-stick skillet over medium-high heat. When the skillet is heated, put the skin-side-down salmon fillets.
3. Cook for about 4-5 minutes on the skin side, until the skin is crisp and golden. Flip the fillets and cook for another 2-4 minutes, or until the salmon reaches your desired doneness. Remove from the skillet and let it rest.
4. Make the mango salsa while the fish cooks. Diced mango, red onion, jalapeño, lime juice, chopped cilantro, and diced avocado should all be combined in a medium-sized bowl.
5. Gently toss to mix all the ingredients. Season with a pinch of salt, adjusting to your taste.
6. Serve the pan-seared salmon fillets with a generous topping of the mango salsa.

**Nutritional Information (per serving):** • Calories: 460 kcal • Protein: 34g • Carbohydrates: 20g

• Fat: 29g (majority being heart-healthy monounsaturated and polyunsaturated fats)

• Saturated Fat: 4g • Cholesterol: 94mg • Sodium: 300mg • Dietary Fiber: 6g

• Sugars: 12g (natural sugars from mango and avocado)

## 12.4 Tuna Quinoa Salad

**Servings: 2 | Preparation Time: 15 minutes | Cooking Time: 15 minutes**

### INGREDIENTS:

- 1 cup (185g) quinoa, rinsed
- 2 cups (480ml) water
- 1 can (around 5 oz or 142g) tuna in water, drained and flaked
- 1/2 cup (90g) cherry tomatoes, halved
- 1/2 cucumber, diced
- 1/4 red onion, finely chopped
- 1/4 cup (15g) fresh parsley, chopped
- 1/4 cup (60ml) extra virgin olive oil
- Juice of 1 lemon
- Salt and pepper to taste

### INSTRUCTIONS:

1. To cook the quinoa, place two cups of water in a small pot and bring to a boil. After rinsing, add the quinoa, lower the heat to a simmer, cover, and cook for about 15 minutes, or until all the water is absorbed. After taking off the heat, let the quinoa cool to room temperature.
2. Combine the chilled quinoa, cucumber, red onion, cherry tomatoes, flaked tuna, and fresh parsley in a sizable mixing dish.
3. To make a simple dressing, mix the extra virgin olive oil and lemon juice together in a small bowl.
4. After adding the dressing to the quinoa salad, toss to coat everything evenly. Adjust the amount of salt and pepper to suit your taste.
5. Serve the salad by dividing it between two bowls or plates. You can enjoy the salad as a light yet protein-rich lunch or as a refreshing side dish.

**Nutritional Information (per serving):** • Calories: 400 kcal • Protein: 24g • Carbohydrates: 40g • Fat: 17g (beneficial fats mainly from olive oil and tuna) • Saturated Fat: 2.5g • Cholesterol: 30mg

• Sodium: 290mg (can vary based on the salt content in the canned tuna and seasoning)

• Dietary Fiber: 5g • Sugars: 3g (natural sugars from the vegetables)

# 12.5 Fish Tacos with Cabbage Slaw

Servings: 2 | Preparation Time: 20 minutes | Cooking Time: 10 minutes

## INGREDIENTS:

### For the Fish:

- 2 white fish fillets (such as cod or tilapia), about 6 oz (170g) each
- 1/2 teaspoon chili powder
- 1/2 teaspoon ground cumin
- 1/2 teaspoon paprika
- 1/4 teaspoon garlic powder
- Salt and pepper to taste
- 1 tablespoon (15ml) olive oil

### For the Cabbage Slaw:

- 2 cups shredded green cabbage
- 1 cup shredded red cabbage
- 1/2 carrot, grated
- 1/4 cup chopped fresh cilantro
- Juice of 1 lime
- 1 tablespoon (15ml) apple cider vinegar
- 1/2 tablespoon (7.5ml) honey
- Salt to taste

### To Serve:

- 4 small whole-grain or corn tortillas
- 1 ripe avocado, sliced
- Extra lime wedges
- Hot sauce (optional)

## INSTRUCTIONS:

1. Preheat a skillet or grill pan on medium-high heat.
2. In a small bowl, stir together the ground cumin, paprika, garlic powder, chili powder, salt, and pepper. Sprinkle this spice mixture evenly over the fish fillets.
3. The seasoned fish fillets should be added to the skillet along with some olive oil. Cook for about 3-5 minutes on each side, depending on thickness, until the fish is opaque and flakes easily with a fork. Remove from heat.
4. Make the cabbage slaw while the fish cooks. Grated carrot, fresh cilantro, and green and red cabbage should all be combined in a big bowl. Mix the lime juice, apple cider vinegar, honey, and a small amount of salt in a different small bowl. Drizzle the cabbage mixture with this dressing, tossing to coat thoroughly.
5. Warm the tortillas in the microwave or on the skillet for a few seconds on each side until heated through.
6. Assemble the tacos by flaking the cooked fish with a fork and distributing it evenly among the tortillas. Top with the cabbage slaw and slices of avocado.
7. If preferred, garnish with additional lime wedges and spicy sauce.

## Nutritional Information (per serving):

- Calories: 470 kcal • Protein: 38g • Carbohydrates: 42g • Fat: 18g (healthy fats from avocado and olive oil)
- Saturated Fat: 3g • Cholesterol: 85mg • Sodium: 230mg • Dietary Fiber: 11g
- Sugars: 9g (mostly from the honey in the slaw dressing)

## 13.1 Chicken Tortilla Soup

**Servings: 2 | Preparation Time: 15 minutes | Cooking Time: 25 minutes**

### INGREDIENTS:

- 1 tablespoon (15ml) olive oil
- 1/2 onion, diced
- 1 small clove garlic, minced
- 1/2 teaspoon ground cumin
- 1/4 teaspoon chili powder
- 1/2 (14.5 oz or 411g) can diced tomatoes, with their juice
- 2 cups (475ml) low-sodium chicken broth
- 1/2 cup (75g) cooked chicken breast, shredded
- 1/4 cup (40g) cooked black beans, drained and rinsed
- 1/2 cup (75g) frozen corn kernels, thawed
- Salt and pepper to taste
- 2 small corn tortillas, cut into strips
- 1 tablespoon (15ml) fresh lime juice

### Optional Toppings:

- Avocado slices
- Shredded cheese
- Fresh cilantro
- Lime wedges
- Diced red onion

### INSTRUCTIONS:

1. In a big pot, warm the olive oil over medium heat. Add the onion and garlic and cook until softened about 3 minutes.
2. Add the diced tomatoes, chili powder, and ground cumin. Simmer for a further 2 minutes to let the flavors combine.
3. After adding the chicken broth, boil the mixture. Add the shredded chicken, black beans, and corn. Season with salt and pepper to taste. Simmer for about 15 minutes.
4. Heat the oven to 375°F (190°C) while the soup is cooking. Place the tortilla strips on a baking pan and bake for 10-15 minutes, or until they are crispy.
5. After taking the soup off of the stove, stir in the lime juice. Adjust seasonings if necessary.
6. Spoon soup into individual bowls and top with crunchy tortilla strips. Add any additional desired toppings, such as avocado slices, shredded cheese, fresh cilantro, lime wedges, or diced red onion.

### Nutritional Information (per serving):

- Calories: 325 kcal • Protein: 22g • Carbohydrates: 33g
- Fat: 13g (primarily from the olive oil, which contains heart-healthy monounsaturated fats)
- Saturated Fat: 2g • Cholesterol: 45mg • Sodium: 410mg (may vary if additional salt is added)
- Dietary Fiber: 6g • Sugars: 6g (natural sugars from the vegetables)

# 13.2 Turkey Meatball Subs with Marinara

Servings: 2 | Preparation Time: 20 minutes | Cooking Time: 20 minutes

## INGREDIENTS:

### For the Mini Turkey Meatballs:

- 1/2 pound (225g) ground turkey
- 2 tablespoons (12.5g) breadcrumbs
- 2 tablespoons (15g) grated Parmesan cheese
- 1/2 large egg, beaten
- 1 clove garlic, minced

- 1/2 tablespoon chopped fresh parsley
- 1/4 teaspoon dried oregano
- Salt and pepper to taste
- 1/2 tablespoon olive oil, for cooking

### For the Marinara Sauce:

- 1/2 tablespoon olive oil
- 1/2 small onion, finely chopped
- 1 clove garlic, minced
- 1/2 can (7 oz / 200g) crushed tomatoes

- 1/2 teaspoon dried basil
- 1/2 teaspoon dried oregano
- Salt and pepper to taste

### To Serve:

- 2 whole-grain sub rolls
- 1/4 cup shredded mozzarella cheese (optional)

## INSTRUCTIONS:

### For the Mini Turkey Meatballs:

1. Preheat your oven to 400°F (200°C). Paper or aluminum foil should be used to line a baking pan.
2. Combine grated Parmesan cheese, breadcrumbs, ground turkey, beaten egg, minced garlic, chopped fresh parsley, dried oregano, and salt and pepper to taste in a large mixing bowl. Mix until well combined.
3. Form the turkey mixture into tiny meatballs, no more than an inch around, and arrange them on the baking sheet that has been preheated.
4. Bake for 15 to 20 minutes, or until the meatballs are cooked through and have a light brown color, in a preheated oven.

### For the Marinara Sauce:

1. Grease a medium pot with olive oil and preheat it while the meatballs bake.
2. Add the finely chopped onion and sauté for 3–4 minutes or until softened.
3. Add the minced garlic and stir. Cook for an extra minute, or until fragrant.
4. Add the crushed tomatoes, dried basil, and dried oregano to the saucepan. Season with salt and pepper to taste, and let the sauce simmer for about 10 minutes, until heated through and slightly thickened.

### To Assemble the Subs:

1. Slice the whole-grain sub rolls open, being careful not to cut all the way through.
2. Place an even amount of turkey meatballs inside each roll.
3. Spoon the marinara sauce over the meatballs.
4. Sprinkle with shredded mozzarella cheese, if using.
5. Place the subs back in the oven for a few minutes until the cheese is melted and the bread is slightly toasted.

**Nutritional Information (per serving):** • Calories: 480 kcal • Protein: 35g • Carbohydrates: 45g • Fat: 18g (healthy fats from olive oil and ground turkey) • Saturated Fat: 4.5g • Cholesterol: 95mg • Sodium: 790mg
• Dietary Fiber: 6g • Sugars: 8g (mostly from tomatoes in marinara sauce)

# 13.3 Orange Glazed Chicken Stir-Fry

**Servings: 2 | Preparation Time: 20 minutes | Cooking Time: 15 minutes**

## INGREDIENTS:

### For the Stir-Fry:
- 2 boneless, skinless chicken breasts (about 1/2 pound or 225g), cut into bite-size pieces
- 1 tablespoon (15ml) olive oil
- 1 bell pepper, sliced into strips
- 1/2 small red onion, sliced
- 1 medium carrot, julienned
- 1/2 cup (75g) sugar snap peas or snow peas

### For the Orange Glaze:
- Zest and juice of 1 large orange
- 1 tablespoon (15ml) soy sauce (low sodium)
- 1 tablespoon (15ml) rice vinegar
- 1 teaspoon (5g) honey
- 1 small clove garlic, minced
- 1/2 teaspoon (2g) grated fresh ginger
- 1/2 tablespoon (4g) cornstarch mixed with 1 tablespoon (15ml) water

### To Serve:
- Cooked brown rice or quinoa
- Sesame seeds (optional)
- Sliced green onions (optional)

## INSTRUCTIONS:

1. To make the orange glaze, combine the orange zest and juice, soy sauce, rice vinegar, honey, garlic, and ginger in a small bowl. Set this mixture aside.
2. To thicken the glaze later on, mix the cornstarch and water in a separate small bowl to create a slurry.
3. On medium-high heat, warm the olive oil in a big skillet or wok. Add the chicken pieces and stir-fry until browned and nearly cooked through, about 5-7 minutes.
4. Add the sliced bell pepper, red onion, julienned carrot, and sugar snap peas to the skillet with the chicken. Stir-fry the vegetables with the chicken until they are crisp-tender, about 3-4 minutes.
5. After lowering the heat to medium, cover the chicken and vegetables with the orange glaze. Stir the glaze through to coat everything evenly.
6. Add the cornstarch slurry and heat for an additional 2-3 minutes, or until the chicken is cooked through and the glaze has slightly thickened.
7. Serve the orange glazed chicken stir-fry hot over cooked brown rice or quinoa. If preferred, add sliced green onions and sesame seeds as garnish.

## Nutritional Information (per serving):

- Calories: 350 kcal • Protein: 27g • Carbohydrates: 28g
- Fat: 14g (the majority from olive oil, which contains heart-healthy monounsaturated fats)
- Saturated Fat: 2g • Cholesterol: 65mg • Sodium: 460mg (varies if low-sodium soy sauce is used)
- Dietary Fiber: 4g • Sugars: 12g (natural sugars from the orange juice and honey)

## 13.4 Balsamic Glazed Turkey Breast

Servings: 2 | Preparation Time: 10 minutes | Cooking Time: 30 minutes

### INGREDIENTS:

- 1 pound (450g) turkey breast cutlets
- Salt and pepper to taste
- 1 tablespoon (15ml) olive oil
- 2 tablespoons (30ml) balsamic vinegar
- 1 tablespoon (15ml) honey
- 1 clove garlic, minced
- 1 teaspoon (5ml) Dijon mustard
- A pinch of dried thyme or 1 teaspoon (5ml) fresh thyme leaves
- Optional: Fresh herbs (rosemary, thyme) for garnish

### INSTRUCTIONS:

1. Season the turkey breast cutlets with salt and pepper on both sides.
2. In a big skillet, warm the olive oil over medium-high heat. Once hot, add the turkey cutlets and cook for about 4-5 minutes on each side, or until they are golden brown and cooked through. To keep the cutlets warm, move them on a platter and cover them with foil.
3. In the same skillet, reduce the heat to medium and add the balsamic vinegar, honey, minced garlic, Dijon mustard, and thyme. Cook, stirring, for 2-3 minutes, or until the sauce becomes slightly thicker and becomes a glaze.
4. Return the turkey cutlets to the pan, spooning the balsamic glaze over them to coat them thoroughly. Cook for another 1-2 minutes, ensuring the turkey is well-glazed and heated through.
5. Transfer the glazed turkey cutlets to serving plates. Add some fresh herbs, such as thyme or rosemary, as a garnish for a fragrant and savory presentation.

### Nutritional Information (per serving):

• Calories: 360 kcal • Protein: 48g • Carbohydrates: 14g • Fat: 11g (healthy fats from olive oil)

• Saturated Fat: 1.5g • Cholesterol: 100mg • Sodium: 330mg • Dietary Fiber: 0g

• Sugars: 13g (natural sugars from honey)

## 13.5 Chicken Waldorf Salad

Servings: 2 | Preparation Time: 15 minutes | Cooking Time: 15 minutes (for chicken, if not using pre-cooked)

### INGREDIENTS:

- 1 cup (150g) cooked chicken breast, diced
- 1/2 cup (60g) celery, diced
- 1/2 cup (60g) red apple, diced
- 1/4 cup (30g) red grapes, halved
- 1/4 cup (30g) walnuts, chopped
- 1/4 cup (60ml) plain Greek yogurt
- 1 tablespoon (15ml) mayonnaise
- 1 tablespoon (15ml) lemon juice
- 1 tablespoon (15ml) honey
- Salt and pepper to taste
- Lettuce leaves, for serving (optional)

## INSTRUCTIONS:

1. Diced chicken breast, diced celery, diced red apple, half-red grapes, and chopped walnuts should all be combined in a big mixing bowl.
2. Mayonnaise, lemon juice, honey, plain Greek yogurt, salt, and pepper should all be thoroughly mixed together in a small bowl.
3. Pour the dressing over the chicken salad mixture in the big bowl. Toss until everything is evenly coated with the dressing.
4. After tasting the Waldorf Chicken Salad, taste it again and adjust the seasoning by adding extra honey, lemon juice, salt, or pepper to suit your tastes.
5. Serve the salad chilled on a bed of lettuce leaves, if you like, for an added crunch and a beautiful presentation.

**Nutritional Information (per serving):**

• Calories: 380 kcal • Protein: 25g • Carbohydrates: 20g • Fat: 22g • Saturated Fat: 4g • Cholesterol: 80mg
• Sodium: 450mg • Fiber: 5g • Sugar: 12g

# Chapter 14: Meaty Must-Haves

## 14.1 Sirloin Steak with Roasted Vegetables

Servings: 2 | Preparation Time: 15 minutes | Cooking Time: 25 minutes

### INGREDIENTS:

- 8 ounces (225g) sirloin steak
- 1 tablespoon (15ml) olive oil, divided
- Salt and pepper to taste
- 1/2 cup (75g) cherry tomatoes, halved
- 1 medium zucchini, cut into half-moons
- 1 red bell pepper, cut into 1-inch pieces
- 1/2 red onion, cut into wedges
- 2 cloves garlic, minced
- 1 teaspoon (5ml) balsamic vinegar
- 1/2 teaspoon (1g) dried oregano
- 1/2 teaspoon (1g) dried thyme

### INSTRUCTIONS:

1. Preheat your oven to 425°F (220°C). Toss the cherry tomatoes, zucchini, bell pepper, and red onion with half of the olive oil, balsamic vinegar, oregano, thyme, salt, and pepper in a large bowl.
2. Spread the vegetables out on a baking sheet in a single layer and roast in the preheated oven for about 20-25 minutes or until they are caramelized and tender, stirring halfway through cooking time.
3. Meanwhile, in a big skillet set over medium-high heat, warm the remaining olive oil. Season the sirloin steak with salt and pepper on both sides.
4. After the skillet is hot, place the steak inside and cook it for about 4–5 minutes on each side, or until it is cooked to your preferred doneness. Before slicing, let the steak rest for a few minutes.
5. Serve the sliced steak with the roasted vegetables on the side. Drizzle the vegetables with any remaining balsamic and olive oil mix and sprinkle with the minced garlic for added flavor.

**Nutritional Information (per serving):** • Calories: 400 kcal • Protein: 35g • Carbohydrates: 20g • Sugars: 8g (natural sugars from vegetables) • Fat: 20g (predominantly from olive oil, a source of heart-healthy monounsaturated fats) • Saturated Fat: 4.5g • Cholesterol: 90mg • Sodium: 300mg • Dietary Fiber: 4g

## 14.2 Beef and Broccoli Stir Fry

**Servings: 2 | Preparation Time: 10 minutes | Cooking Time: 15 minutes**

### INGREDIENTS:

- 8 ounces (225g) lean beef (such as flank steak), thinly sliced
- 2 cups (180g) broccoli florets
- 1 tablespoon (15ml) vegetable oil
- 2 cloves garlic, minced
- 1 teaspoon fresh ginger, grated
- 1/4 cup (60ml) low-sodium soy sauce or tamari for a gluten-free option
- 1 tablespoon (15ml) oyster sauce (optional)
- 1 tablespoon (15ml) honey
- 1 teaspoon (5ml) cornstarch diluted in 2 tablespoons water
- Sesame seeds, for garnish (optional)
- Cooked brown rice for serving

### INSTRUCTIONS:

1. After 2 minutes of blanching in boiling water, immediately submerge the broccoli florets in freezing water to halt the cooking process. Drain and set aside.
2. Mix the cornstarch mixture, honey, oyster sauce (if using), and soy sauce in a small bowl.
3. In a wok or big skillet, heat the vegetable oil over medium-high heat. Stir-fry the grated ginger and minced garlic for about 30 seconds, or until fragrant.
4. Lean beef slices should be added to the wok and stir-fried for 2-3 minutes, or until they begin to brown.
5. Add the blanched broccoli after pouring in the sauce mixture. Toss everything together and cook for another 2-3 minutes, or until the sauce has thickened and the beef is cooked through.
6. If desired, sprinkle sesame seeds over the stir fry before serving.
7. For a full dinner, serve the stir-fried beef and broccoli over cooked brown rice.

### Nutritional Information (per serving):

- Calories: 330 kcal • Protein: 28g • Carbohydrates: 22g • Fat: 12g • Saturated Fat: 2g • Cholesterol: 70mg
- Sodium: 600mg • Dietary Fiber: 4g • Sugars: 8g (natural sugars from honey and vegetables)

# 14.3 Lamb Kebabs with Mint Yogurt Sauce

**Servings: 2 | Preparation Time: 20 minutes (plus marinating time) | Cooking Time: 10 minutes**

## INGREDIENTS:

- 8 ounces (225g) lean lamb, cut into 1-inch cubes
- 1 red onion, cut into 1-inch pieces
- 1 bell pepper, cut into 1-inch pieces
- 1 zucchini, cut into 1-inch slices
- 2 tablespoons (30ml) olive oil
- 1 teaspoon (2g) ground cumin
- 1 teaspoon (2g) smoked paprika
- Salt and pepper to taste

### For the Mint Yogurt Sauce:

- 1/2 cup (120ml) plain Greek yogurt
- 1 tablespoon (15ml) fresh mint, finely chopped
- 1 clove garlic, minced
- Juice of 1/2 lemon
- Salt to taste

## INSTRUCTIONS:

1. Mix the olive oil, smoked paprika, ground cumin, salt, and pepper in a bowl. Add the lamb cubes to the marinade and toss to coat evenly. Cover and let the lamb marinate in the refrigerator for at least 1 hour.
2. While the lamb is marinating, prepare the mint yogurt sauce by mixing together the plain Greek yogurt, finely chopped mint, minced garlic, lemon juice, and salt in a bowl. Adjust the seasoning if necessary and refrigerate until serving time.
3. Turn the heat up to medium-high on the grill or grill pan.
4. Thread the marinated lamb cubes onto skewers, alternating with pieces of red onion, bell pepper, and zucchini slices.
5. Turning regularly, grill the kebabs for about 10 minutes, or until the lamb is cooked to your preference and the veggies are soft and gently browned.
6. Serve the lamb kebabs with a generous dollop of the mint yogurt sauce on the side or drizzled over the top.

## Nutritional Information (per serving):

- Calories: 390 kcal • Protein: 26g • Carbohydrates: 15g
- Fat: 25g (predominantly from olive oil and lean lamb, providing healthy monounsaturated fats)
- Saturated Fat: 6g • Cholesterol: 80mg • Sodium: 250mg • Dietary Fiber: 3g • Sugars: 8g

# 14.4 Meatballs with Tomato Sauce and Spaghetti Squash

**Servings: 2 | Preparation Time: 20 minutes | Cooking Time: 60 minutes**

## INGREDIENTS:

### For the Meatballs:
- 8 ounces (225g) ground turkey
- 1/4 cup (25g) breadcrumbs
- 1 egg
- 2 tablespoons (30g) grated Parmesan cheese
- 1 clove garlic, minced
- 1 tablespoon fresh parsley, chopped
- 1/2 teaspoon dried oregano
- Salt and pepper to taste

### For the Tomato Sauce:
- 1 tablespoon (15ml) olive oil
- 1/2 cup (120ml) diced onion
- 1 clove garlic, minced
- 1 can (14 oz / 400g) crushed tomatoes
- 1 teaspoon dried basil
- Salt and pepper to taste

### For the Spaghetti Squash:
- 1 small spaghetti squash (about 2 pounds / 900g)

## INSTRUCTIONS:

1. Preheat the oven to 400°F (200°C). Scoop out the seeds after cutting the spaghetti squash in half lengthwise.
2. On a baking sheet, place the halves of the squash cut side down. Roast for 40 to 45 minutes or until the flesh is soft and flakeable with a fork.
3. Meanwhile, the squash is roasting. Combine the ground turkey, breadcrumbs, egg, Parmesan cheese, minced garlic, chopped parsley, dried oregano, salt, and pepper in a basin. Mix until well incorporated.
4. Once the mixture is formed into tiny meatballs with a diameter of approximately an inch, put them on a baking sheet that has been buttered.
5. Bake for 15 to 20 minutes, or until the meatballs are thoroughly cooked, in an oven that has been warmed.
6. Meanwhile, place a saucepan over medium heat with the olive oil. Sauté the minced garlic and diced onion for 3-4 minutes or until the ingredients are tender. Add crushed tomatoes and dried basil. After adding salt and pepper to taste, boil it for around fifteen minutes.
7. After cooking, take the squash out of the oven and allow it to cool somewhat. Scoop out the flesh from the inside of the squash with a fork so that it resembles spaghetti.
8. Serve the spaghetti squash on plates and top with warm tomato sauce and meatballs. If desired, add more grated Parmesan cheese as a garnish.

## Nutritional Information (per serving):

- Calories: 480 kcal • Protein: 36g • Carbohydrates: 50g • Fat: 16g • Saturated Fat: 4g • Cholesterol: 162mg
- Sodium: 540mg • Dietary Fiber: 6g • Sugars: 8g

# 14.5 Slow Cooker Pulled Pork with Slaw

Servings: 2 | Preparation Time: 15 minutes | Cooking Time: 8 hours (slow cooker on low)

## INGREDIENTS:

### For the Pulled Pork:

- 1 pound (450g) pork tenderloin
- 1/2 cup (120ml) low-sodium chicken broth
- 1/2 cup (120ml) apple cider vinegar
- 1 tablespoon (15g) honey
- 1 teaspoon smoked paprika
- 1 teaspoon garlic powder
- 1/2 teaspoon ground cumin
- 1/2 teaspoon onion powder
- Salt and pepper to taste
- Whole grain buns (optional, for serving)

### For the Slaw:

- 2 cups (150g) shredded cabbage (mix of red and green)
- 1 medium carrot, shredded
- 1/4 cup (60ml) plain Greek yogurt
- 1 tablespoon (15ml) apple cider vinegar
- 1 tablespoon (15g) Dijon mustard
- 1 teaspoon honey
- Salt and pepper to taste

## INSTRUCTIONS:

1. Stir together the onion powder, ground cumin, garlic powder, honey, apple cider vinegar, smoked paprika, salt, and pepper in the slow cooker with the chicken broth.
2. Toss the pork tenderloin around in the sauce after adding it to the slow cooker.
3. For around 8 hours, cook on low with a lid on. The pork should be very tender and easy to shred.
4. Using two forks, shred the cooked pork after taking it out of the slow cooker.
5. Coat and reheat the pulled pork by combining it with the sauce once more in the slow cooker.
6. To prepare the slaw, mix the shredded cabbage and carrot in a bowl. Mix the Greek yogurt, honey, Dijon mustard, apple cider vinegar, salt, and pepper in a separate bowl to make the dressing.
7. Drizzle the cabbage mixture with the dressing, then toss to mix. Let it sit for at least 10 minutes for the flavors to meld.
8. For a low-carb version, top the pulled pork with a generous amount of slaw and serve it on whole-grain buns with an additional side of slaw.

## Nutritional Information (per serving, without buns):

• Calories: 410 kcal • Protein: 52g • Carbohydrates: 22g • Fat: 12g • Saturated Fat: 3g • Cholesterol: 145mg
• Sodium: 320mg • Dietary Fiber: 3g • Sugars: 18g

# Chapter 15: Sugar-Free Sweets

## 15.1 Baked Apples with Oat Crumble

Servings: 2 | Preparation Time: 10 minutes | Baking Time: 30 minutes

### INGREDIENTS:

**For the Baked Apples:**

*   2 large apples, such as Honeycrisp or Granny Smith, cored
*   1/4 cup (60ml) apple cider or water
*   1/2 teaspoon (1g) ground cinnamon
*   1/4 teaspoon (0.5g) ground nutmeg

**For the Oat Crumble:**

*   1/2 cup (40g) rolled oats
*   2 tablespoons (16g) whole wheat flour
*   1 tablespoon (15g) cold unsalted butter, diced
*   1 tablespoon (15ml) maple syrup or honey
*   1/4 teaspoon (1g) ground cinnamon
*   A pinch of salt

### INSTRUCTIONS:

1.  Preheat the oven to 375°F (190°C).
2.  Put the apples that have been cored onto a small baking dish. Pour the apple cider or water into the bottom of the dish, and sprinkle the apples with cinnamon and nutmeg.
3.  In a bowl, combine rolled oats, whole wheat flour, cinnamon, and salt. Add the cold butter pieces and maple syrup or honey. Use your fingers or a fork to mix until the mixture becomes crumbly.
4.  Spoon the oat crumble mixture into the center of the apples, packing it down lightly and then mounding it on top.
5.  When a knife pierces the apples, they should be prepared, and the crumble should be golden brown (after about 30 minutes of baking in a preheated oven).
6.  Allow to cool for a few minutes before serving. If desired, drizzle with a little extra maple syrup or honey, or top with a dollop of Greek yogurt.

### Nutritional Information (per serving):

• Calories: 200 kcal • Protein: 2g • Carbohydrates: 42g • Fat: 4g • Saturated Fat: 2g • Cholesterol: 10mg
• Sodium: 55mg • Dietary Fiber: 6g • Sugars: 28g (natural sugars from apples and added sweeteners)

## 15.2 Almond Joy Energy Balls

Servings: 2 (6 balls per serving) | Preparation Time: 15 minutes | Chill Time: 30 minutes

### INGREDIENTS:

*   1/2 cup (45g) rolled oats
*   1/4 cup (20g) unsweetened shredded coconut
*   1/4 cup (35g) whole almonds
*   2 tablespoons (15g) cocoa powder
*   1/4 cup (60ml) almond butter
*   2 tablespoons (30ml) honey or maple syrup
*   1/2 teaspoon (2.5ml) vanilla extract
*   A pinch of salt
*   2 tablespoons (30ml) water, if needed to bind

## INSTRUCTIONS:

1. To make the mixture crumbly, pulse the rolled oats, shredded coconut, whole almonds, and cocoa powder in a food processor.
2. Transfer the almond butter, vanilla extract, honey (or maple syrup), and a small amount of salt into the food processor.
3. Pulse until the mixture starts to come together. If the mixture is too dry, add a little water, one tablespoon at a time, until the mixture is sticky enough to hold together.
4. Using clean hands, take small scoops of the mixture and roll into 1-inch balls. You should be able to make around 12 balls.
5. Place the energy balls on a parchment-lined tray or plate and chill in the refrigerator for at least 30 minutes to help them set.
6. The Almond Joy Energy Balls can be enjoyed right away when they're cold and hard, or they can be kept in the refrigerator for up to a week in an airtight container.

### Nutritional Information (per serving):

- Calories: 280 kcal • Protein: 8g • Carbohydrates: 28g • Fat: 16g • Saturated Fat: 3g • Cholesterol: 0mg
- Sodium: 80mg • Dietary Fiber: 5g • Sugars: 12g

## 15.3 Poached Pears in Red Wine

**Servings: 2 | Preparation Time: 10 minutes | Cook Time: 25-30 minutes**

### INGREDIENTS:

- 2 ripe pears, peeled, halved, and cored
- 1 cup (240ml) red wine (choose one that's relatively low in sugar)
- 1/4 cup (50g) honey or to taste (you can adjust based on the sweetness you desire)
- 1 cinnamon stick
- 2 cloves
- 1 strip of orange zest (about 2 inches long)
- 1/2 vanilla pod, split lengthwise (or 1 teaspoon vanilla extract)

### INSTRUCTIONS:

1. In a saucepan that's just large enough to fit the pear halves, combine the red wine, honey, cinnamon stick, cloves, orange zest, and vanilla pod over medium heat.
2. Simmer, stirring now and again, until the honey dissolves completely into the wine.
3. Carefully place the pear halves into the saucepan in a single layer.
4. Bring the wine mixture to a low simmer and cover the pan with a lid.
5. Allow the pears to poach gently, turning once or twice, until they are just tender but not mushy, about 25-30 minutes. The variety and level of ripeness of the pears will determine the precise time.
6. With a slotted spoon, remove and place the pears aside. They can be served warm or chilled.
7. Continue to simmer the wine sauce uncovered to reduce it to a syrupy consistency, about 10-15 minutes. Remove the spices and orange zest.
8. If serving the poached pears chilled, refrigerate both the pears and the sauce until cooled.
9. To present, pour the wine reduction over the poached pears and serve with low-fat whipped cream or a dollop of Greek yogurt, if preferred.

### Nutritional Information (per serving):

- Calories: 310 kcal • Protein: 1g • Carbohydrates: 45g • Fat: 0g • Saturated Fat: 0g • Cholesterol: 0mg
- Sodium: 5mg • Dietary Fiber: 5g • Sugars: 35g

# 15.4 Blueberry Almond Crisp

Servings: 2 | Preparation Time: 15 minutes | Baking Time: 30-35 minutes

## INGREDIENTS:

### For the Blueberry Filling:

- 2 cups mixed berries (such as blueberries, raspberries, and blackberries)
- 1/8 cup (25g) granulated sugar
- 1/2 tablespoon (4g) cornstarch
- 1/2 tablespoon (7.5ml) lemon juice
- Zest of 1/2 lemon

### For the Almond Crisp Topping:

- 1/2 cup (45g) old-fashioned rolled oats
- 1/4 cup (30g) all-purpose flour
- 1/4 cup (25g) sliced almonds
- 1/4 cup (50g) brown sugar
- 1/4 teaspoon (1.25g) ground cinnamon
- 1/8 teaspoon (0.5g) salt
- 1/4 cup (57.5g) unsalted butter, melted

## INSTRUCTIONS:

1. Preheat the oven to 350°F (175°C). Grease a small baking dish appropriate for two servings.
2. In a large mixing basin, combine the mixed berries, zest, cornstarch, lemon juice, and granulated sugar. After tossing the berries to coat them evenly, put the mixture into the baking dish that has been prepared and spread it out evenly.
3. For the almond crisp topping, put the flour, sliced almonds, brown sugar, ground cinnamon, and salt in a separate mixing bowl. Mix well.
4. Pour the melted unsalted butter over the oat mixture and stir until the ingredients are well blended and moistened.
5. Sprinkle the almond crisp topping evenly over the berry filling in the baking dish.
6. Bake for about 30 to 35 minutes in a preheated oven or until the berry filling is bubbling and the topping is golden brown.
7. Let the crisp cool slightly before serving. It may be served warm or at room temperature, and for extra sweetness, you can top it with a drizzle of honey or a dollop of Greek yogurt.

## Nutritional Information (per serving):

• Calories: 520 kcal • Protein: 7g • Carbohydrates: 68g • Fat: 26g • Saturated Fat: 12g • Cholesterol: 48mg
• Sodium: 150mg • Dietary Fiber: 8g • Sugars: 38g

# 15.5 Raspberry Lemon Cheesecake Cups

**Servings: 2 | Preparation Time: 20 minutes | Chilling Time: 2 hours**

## INGREDIENTS:

### For the Cheesecake Filling:

- 4 ounces (113g) reduced-fat cream cheese, softened
- 1/4 cup (60g) plain Greek yogurt
- 2 tablespoons (30ml) honey or maple syrup
- 1/2 teaspoon (2.5ml) vanilla extract
- Zest of 1 lemon
- 1 tablespoon (15ml) lemon juice

### For the Raspberry Sauce:

- 1 cup (about 150g) fresh raspberries
- 1 tablespoon (15g) granulated sugar
- 1 tablespoon (15ml) water

### For the Crust:

- 1/4 cup (25g) rolled oats
- 2 tablespoons (16g) almond meal or ground almonds
- 1 tablespoon (15g) unsalted butter, melted
- 1 tablespoon (15g) honey or maple syrup

## INSTRUCTIONS:

1. Mix rolled oats, almond meal, melted butter, and honey or maple syrup in a bowl until well combined to prepare the crust. Press the mixture into the bottom of two serving cups or small jars, creating a crust layer. While making the filling, let it cool in the refrigerator.

2. Cream cheese that has softened, Greek yogurt, honey or maple syrup, vanilla extract, zest from lemons, and lemon juice should all be combined in a separate mixing dish and beaten until smooth and creamy.

3. In each cup, spoon or pipe the cheesecake filling over the crust. Smooth out the top with a spoon or spatula.

4. Put the raspberries, sugar, and water in a small saucepan to prepare the raspberry sauce. Simmer the raspberries over medium heat, stirring periodically, for 5 to 7 minutes or until the sauce starts to thicken. If preferred, strain the sauce through a fine-mesh strainer to get rid of the seeds.

5. Allow the raspberry sauce to cool, then spoon it over the cheesecake filling in each cup.

6. Refrigerate the cheesecake cups for at least 2 hours or until they are set and chilled.

7. If preferred, garnish before serving with more fresh raspberries and a sprig of fresh mint.

## Nutritional Information (per serving):

• Calories: 300 kcal • Protein: 8g • Carbohydrates: 34g • Fat: 16g • Saturated Fat: 8g • Cholesterol: 30mg
• Sodium: 180mg • Dietary Fiber: 4g • Sugars: 26g

# Chapter 16: Wholesome Breads

## 16.1 Multigrain Loaf

**Servings: 2 (6 slices per serving) | Preparation Time: 2 hours (including rise time)**
**Cook Time: 35-40 minutes**

### INGREDIENTS:

- 1 cup (240ml) lukewarm water
- 2 teaspoons (7g) active dry yeast
- 1 tablespoon (15ml) honey or maple syrup
- 1 1/2 cups (180g) whole wheat flour
- 1/2 cup (60g) rolled oats
- 1/4 cup (30g) millet
- 2 tablespoons (16g) flaxseeds
- 2 tablespoons (14g) sunflower seeds
- 1 tablespoon (9g) sesame seeds
- 1 teaspoon (5g) salt
- 1 tablespoon (15ml) olive oil

### INSTRUCTIONS:

1. Mix the lukewarm water with the honey (or maple syrup) and yeast in a small basin. Allow it to sit for five to ten minutes or until foamy, which is a sign of active yeast.

2. The whole wheat flour, rolled oats, millet, sesame seeds, sunflower seeds, flaxseeds, and salt should all be combined in a big mixing basin.

3. Mix in the olive oil and the foamy yeast mixture with the dry ingredients until a dough forms.

4. Work the dough for approximately 10 minutes on a floured board or until it is elastic and smooth. For this task, a stand mixer with a dough hook attached is another option.

5. Place the kneaded dough in a greased bowl, cover it with a damp cloth, and let it rise in a warm place for about 1 hour or until it doubles in size.

6. After pounding the dough into a loaf form, place it in a buttered loaf pan. Cover it again and let it rise for an additional 30 minutes.

7. Preheat your oven to 375°F (190°C).

8. When the dough has risen, bake the loaf for 35 to 40 minutes in a preheated oven or until it sounds hollow when tapped on the bottom and has a golden brown top.

9. Before slicing, take the loaf out of the oven and let it cool on a wire rack.

### Nutritional Information (per serving):

• Calories: 260 kcal • Protein: 10g • Carbohydrates: 48g • Fat: 5g • Saturated Fat: 0.5g • Cholesterol: 0mg
• Sodium: 290mg • Dietary Fiber: 9g • Sugars: 4g

# 16.2 Whole Wheat Banana Bread

**Servings: 2 (6 slices per serving) | Preparation Time: 15 minutes | Cook Time: 55-60 minutes**

## INGREDIENTS:

- 1 3/4 cups whole wheat flour
- 1 teaspoon baking soda
- 1/2 teaspoon salt
- 1/2 teaspoon ground cinnamon
- 1/3 cup olive oil or melted coconut oil
- 1/2 cup honey or maple syrup
- 2 eggs
- 1 cup mashed ripe bananas (about 2-3 medium bananas)
- 1/4 cup milk (or a non-dairy alternative like almond milk)
- 1 teaspoon vanilla extract
- 1/2 cup walnuts or pecans, chopped (optional)

## INSTRUCTIONS:

1. Preheat your oven to 325°F (163°C).
2. In a large mixing bowl, mix together the whole wheat flour, baking soda, salt, and ground cinnamon.
3. Mix the oil, eggs, mashed bananas, milk, vanilla extract, honey or maple syrup, and other ingredients in a separate bowl.
4. Stir the mixture just until fully blended after adding the wet components to the dry ingredients. If using, fold in the chopped nuts.
5. A 9 × 5-inch loaf pan can be lined with parchment paper or greased. After the loaf pan is ready, pour the batter into it and distribute it evenly.
6. A toothpick put into the center should come out clean after baking for 55 to 60 minutes in a preheated oven.
7. After letting the bread sit in the pan for 10 minutes, move it to a wire rack to finish cooling before slicing.

## Nutritional Information (per serving):

• Calories: 310 kcal • Protein: 7g • Carbohydrates: 47g • Fat: 12g • Saturated Fat: 1.5g • Cholesterol: 62mg

• Sodium: 330mg • Dietary Fiber: 5g • Sugars: 18g

## 16.3 Pita Bread with Whole Wheat

Servings: 2 (6 pitas per serving) | Preparation Time: 20 minutes | Cook Time: 6-8 minutes per batch

**INGREDIENTS:**

- 1 cup warm water (around 110°F or 45°C)
- 2 teaspoons (7g) active dry yeast
- 1 tablespoon (15ml) olive oil
- 2 1/2 cups (300g) whole wheat flour
- 1 teaspoon (5g) salt
- Extra olive oil for greasing the bowl

**INSTRUCTIONS:**

1. In a small bowl, mix the warm water and olive oil with the dry yeast. Let it sit for about 5 minutes, or until it's frothy.
2. In a large mixing basin, mix together the whole wheat flour and salt.
3. Create a well in the center of the flour mixture and pour in the frothy yeast mixture.
4. After mixing until a shaggy dough forms, knead the dough for 5-7 minutes, either in the bowl or on a lightly floured board, or until it becomes soft and elastic.
5. Spread some olive oil in a clean basin, transfer the dough to it, and cover it with plastic wrap or a moist dish towel. Let it rise in a warm location for one to one and a half hours or until it has doubled in size.
6. Punch down any remaining air bubbles in the dough and divide it into 12 equal pieces once it has risen.
7. Each component should be rolled into a ball and then flattened into a disk with a diameter of roughly 6 inches.
8. Heat a griddle or skillet to a medium-high temperature. Ensure it's hot before you start cooking the pitas.
9. Cook each pita one at a time for about 2-3 minutes on one side until it puffs up, then flip and cook for another 2-3 minutes on the other side.
10. Until you're ready to serve, keep the cooked pitas warm and soft by wrapping them in a fresh dish towel.

**Nutritional Information (per serving):** • Calories: 300 kcal • Protein: 9g • Carbohydrates: 60g • Fat: 4g • Saturated Fat: 0.5g • Cholesterol: 0mg • Sodium: 450mg • Dietary Fiber: 9g • Sugars: 0g

## 16.4 Spiced Pumpkin Bread

Servings: 2 (6 slices per serving) | Preparation Time: 15 minutes | Cook Time: 55-65 minutes

**INGREDIENTS:**

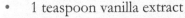

- 1 and 3/4 cups (220g) whole wheat flour
- 1 teaspoon baking powder
- 1/2 teaspoon baking soda
- 1/2 teaspoon salt
- 2 teaspoons ground cinnamon
- 1/2 teaspoon ground nutmeg
- 1/4 teaspoon ground cloves
- 1/4 teaspoon ground ginger
- 1 cup (240g) pumpkin puree (not pumpkin pie filling)
- 1/2 cup (120ml) olive oil or melted coconut oil
- 2 large eggs
- 1/2 cup (100g) granulated sugar
- 1/2 cup (100g) packed brown sugar
- 1 teaspoon vanilla extract
- Optional: 1/2 cup (60g) walnuts or pecans, chopped

## INSTRUCTIONS:

1. Preheat your oven to 350°F (177°C). An 8x4-inch loaf pan can be lined with parchment paper or greased and floured.

2. Blend together the whole wheat flour, baking soda, nutmeg, cinnamon, cloves, and ginger in a big basin.

3. Mix the pumpkin puree, oil, eggs, brown sugar, granulated sugar, and vanilla extract thoroughly in a different bowl.

4. Whisk just till mixed after adding the wet components to the dry ingredients. If desired, fold in the chopped nuts.

5. Using a spatula, level the top of the batter after pouring it into the prepared loaf pan.

6. A toothpick or cake tester placed into the center should come out clean after baking for 55 to 65 minutes in a preheated oven.

7. After letting the bread cool in the pan for 10 minutes, take it out and let it rest fully on a wire rack before slicing it.

**Nutritional Information (per serving):**

• Calories: 330 kcal • Protein: 6g • Carbohydrates: 53g • Fat: 12g • Saturated Fat: 2g • Cholesterol: 62mg
• Sodium: 320mg • Dietary Fiber: 5g • Sugars: 28g

## 16.5 Gluten-Free Cornbread

**Servings: 2 (6 pieces per serving) | Preparation Time: 10 minutes | Cook Time: 20-25 minutes**

## INGREDIENTS:

• 1 cup (120g) gluten-free all-purpose flour
• 1 cup (170g) yellow cornmeal
• 1/4 cup (50g) granulated sugar
• 1 tablespoon (15g) baking powder
• 1/2 teaspoon salt
• 1 cup (240ml) milk (or non-dairy milk for lactose intolerance)
• 1/4 cup (60ml) vegetable oil
• 2 large eggs

## INSTRUCTIONS:

1. Preheat your oven to 375°F (190°C). An 8-inch square baking pan can be lined with parchment paper or greased.

2. Mix the cornmeal, sugar, baking powder, salt, and gluten-free all-purpose flour in a big basin.

3. Blend the eggs, vegetable oil, and milk thoroughly in another bowl.

4. Mixing until just blended, add the wet ingredients to the dry components. Do not overmix.

5. Evenly distribute the batter after pouring it into the pan.

6. A toothpick put into the center of the cornbread should come out clean or with a few wet crumbs after 20 to 25 minutes of baking in a preheated oven or until the top is brown.

7. Take it out of the oven, let it cool in the pan for a few minutes, and then place it on a wire rack to cool down a little bit before serving.

**Nutritional Information (per serving):** • Calories: 290 kcal • Protein: 5g • Carbohydrates: 45g • Fat: 10g

• Saturated Fat: 2g • Cholesterol: 93mg • Sodium: 410mg • Dietary Fiber: 4g • Sugars: 10g

# Chapter 17: Refreshing Drinks

## 17.1 Strawberry Kiwi Water Infusion

Servings: 2 | Preparation Time: 5 minutes | Infusing Time: 2-4 hours

**INGREDIENTS:**

- 4 cups (960ml) cold water
- 1/2 cup (90g) strawberries, hulled and halved
- 1 kiwi, peeled and sliced
- Ice cubes (optional)
- Fresh mint leaves for garnish (optional)

**INSTRUCTIONS:**

1. Fill a large pitcher with 4 cups of cold water.
2. Add the halved strawberries and sliced kiwi to the pitcher.
3. Stir gently to combine the fruits with the water.
4. Place the pitcher in the refrigerator and let the water infuse for 2-4 hours to allow the flavors to meld. You can keep it in the fridge for longer if you'd like a stronger infusion.
5. Before serving, you may add ice cubes to the glasses for an extra cool refreshment.
6. Transfer the infusion of water into glasses and, if preferred, add some fresh mint leaves for a fragrant finishing touch.

**Nutritional Information (per serving):**

• Calories: 30 kcal • Protein: <1g • Carbohydrates: 7g • Fat: <1g • Saturated Fat: 0g • Cholesterol: 0mg
• Sodium: 10mg • Dietary Fiber: 2g • Sugars: 4g

## 17.2 Cucumber Mint Cooler

Servings: 2 | Preparation Time: 10 minutes | Infusing Time: 30 minutes

**INGREDIENTS:**

- 2 cups (about 300g) fresh cucumber, diced
- 1/4 cup (15g) fresh mint leaves
- 2 tablespoons (30ml) lime juice
- 1-2 tablespoons (15-30ml) honey or agave nectar (adjust to taste)
- 2 cups (480ml) cold water
- Ice cubes
- Garnish with cucumber slices and mint sprigs (optional)

**INSTRUCTIONS:**

1. Put the fresh cucumber, mint leaves, and lime juice in a blender.
2. Blend until smooth and well combined.
3. If preferred, strain the mixture into a large pitcher using a fine-mesh sieve to remove the pulp.
4. Stir the agave nectar or honey into the cucumber-mint mixture in the pitcher until it dissolves.
5. Add cold water to the pitcher, and stir to mix thoroughly.
6. If necessary, add extra honey or agave nectar after tasting to adjust the sweetness.
7. Refrigerate the Cucumber Mint Cooler for at least 30 minutes to allow flavors to combine.
8. Serve with ice, garnished with cucumber slices and mint sprigs for a refreshing twist.

**Nutritional Information (per serving):** • Calories: 48 kcal • Protein: 1g • Carbohydrates: 12g • Fat: 0.2g
• Saturated Fat: 0g • Cholesterol: 0mg • Sodium: 3mg • Dietary Fiber: 1g
• Sugars (including natural and added sugars): 9g

# 17.3 Cherry Almond Protein Shake

Servings: 2 | Preparation Time: 5 minutes | Total Time: 5 minutes

## INGREDIENTS:

- 1 cup (240ml) unsweetened almond milk
- 1/2 cup (120ml) cold water
- 1 scoop (approximately 30g) vanilla or plant-based protein powder
- 1 cup (140g) frozen cherries
- 2 tablespoons (30g) natural almond butter
- 1 tablespoon (15ml) honey or maple syrup (optional, depending on desired sweetness)
- Ice cubes (optional)

## INSTRUCTIONS:

1. Add the unsweetened almond milk and cold water to a blender.
2. Incorporate the protein powder, ensuring that it's evenly distributed in the liquid to avoid clumps.
3. Add the frozen cherries and almond butter to the blender.
4. To taste, add honey or maple syrup for a hint of sweetness.
5. Blend the mixture on high until smooth and creamy. If you would like a colder, thicker shake, add a few ice cubes.
6. After tasting the shake, adjust the consistency or sweetness as needed. Add a little more water or almond milk if it's too thick.

Nutritional Information (per serving): • Calories: 215 kcal • Protein: 20g • Carbohydrates: 18g • Fat: 8g
• Saturated Fat: 0.5g • Cholesterol: 0mg • Sodium: 210mg • Dietary Fiber: 3g
• Sugars: 12g (including natural sugars from cherries and optional added honey or maple syrup)

# 17.4 Almond and Date Nighttime Smoothie

Servings: 2 | Preparation Time: 5 minutes | Total Time: 5 minutes

## INGREDIENTS:

- 1 cup (240ml) unsweetened almond milk
- 1/2 cup (120ml) water or additional almond milk
- 1/4 cup (35g) raw almonds, soaked overnight and drained
- 6 pitted dates, preferably Medjool
- 1 ripe banana, sliced and frozen
- 1/2 teaspoon ground cinnamon
- Pinch of nutmeg
- Ice cubes (optional)

## INSTRUCTIONS:

1. Begin by placing the unsweetened almond milk into your blender.
2. Depending on the thickness you want, add more almond milk or water to the smoothie.
3. Incorporate the soaked and drained raw almonds and pitted dates into the blender.
4. Put the frozen sliced banana into the mixture to give the smoothie a creamy texture and natural sweetness.
5. Sprinkle in the ground cinnamon and nutmeg for a warm, soothing flavor that's perfect for nighttime.
6. Feel free to add some ice cubes if you would want your drink to be colder.
7. Blend everything on high until the mixture is smooth and the nuts and dates are fully broken down.
8. Pour into glasses and enjoy immediately for the best quality and taste.

Nutritional Information (per serving): • Calories: 270 kcal • Protein: 6g • Carbohydrates: 8g • Fat: 12g

• Saturated Fat: 1g • Cholesterol: 0mg • Sodium: 80mg • Dietary Fiber: 6g • Sugars: 28g

# 17.5 Green Detox Juice

Servings: 2 | Preparation Time: 10 minutes | Total Time: 10 minutes

## INGREDIENTS:

- 2 cups (60g) fresh spinach leaves
- 1 cup (30g) kale leaves, stems removed
- 1 green apple, cored and sliced
- 1 ripe pear, cored and sliced
- 1 cucumber, sliced
- 1/2 lemon, peeled and seeds removed
- 1-inch piece of ginger, peeled
- 1/2 cup (120ml) cold water or coconut water (adjust according to desired thickness)

## INSTRUCTIONS:

1. Thoroughly wash all the vegetables and fruits. It's important to cleanse them to remove any pesticides and impurities.
2. Prepare the ingredients by cutting the apple and pear into slices, chopping the cucumber, and peeling the lemon and ginger.
3. Place spinach, kale, apple, pear, cucumber, lemon, and ginger in the juicer chute.
4. Start your juicer and begin processing the ingredients. If using a blender, add 1/2 cup of cold water or coconut water to help blend smoothly.
5. If necessary, stop the juicer midway and use a tamper to press the ingredients down.
6. Once everything is juiced, check the consistency, and if needed, add a bit more cold or coconut water to the juicer to thin out the juice.
7. Pour the green detox juice through a fine-mesh strainer if you prefer less pulp.
8. If you would prefer to drink the juice cold, store it in an airtight container in the refrigerator or serve it right away.

## Nutritional Information (per serving):

• Calories: 95 kcal • Protein: 2g • Carbohydrates: 23g • Fat: 0.5g • Saturated Fat: 0g • Cholesterol: 0mg
• Sodium: 60mg • Dietary Fiber: 5g • Sugars: 14g

# Chapter 18: Homemade Condiments

## 18.1 Tomato Salsa Fresca

Servings: 2 | Preparation Time: 15 minutes | Total Time: 15 minutes

**INGREDIENTS:**

- 1 large avocado, diced
- 1 cup (about 200g) cherry tomatoes, quartered
- 1/4 cup (15g) red onion, finely chopped
- 1/4 cup (15g) fresh cilantro, chopped
- 1 lime, juiced
- 1 tablespoon (15ml) extra-virgin olive oil
- Salt and pepper, to taste
- Optional: 1 jalapeño, finely chopped (for added heat)

**INSTRUCTIONS:**

1. Chop the fresh cilantro, finely chop the red onion, dice the avocado, and quarter the cherry tomatoes.
2. Gently combine the diced avocado, quartered cherry tomatoes, chopped red onion, and cilantro in a bowl.
3. Pour the extra virgin olive oil and lime juice over the avocado and tomato combination. Toss gently to coat.
4. To taste, add more pepper and salt to the salsa. Adjust the seasoning as needed.

**Nutritional Information (per serving):** • Calories: 220 kcal • Protein: 3g • Carbohydrates: 20g • Fat: 16g • Saturated Fat: 2g • Cholesterol: 0mg • Sodium: 10mg • Dietary Fiber: 7g • Sugars: 5g

## 18.2 Cilantro Lime Dressing

Servings: 2 | Preparation Time: 5 minutes | Total Time: 5 minutes

**INGREDIENTS:**

- 1/2 cup (8g) fresh cilantro leaves, tightly packed
- Juice of 2 limes (about 1/4 cup or 60ml lime juice)
- 1/4 cup (60ml) extra-virgin olive oil
- 1 garlic clove
- 1 tablespoon (15ml) honey (or agave syrup for vegan option)
- 1/2 teaspoon sea salt
- 1/4 teaspoon black pepper
- 2-3 tablespoons (30-45ml) water, as needed for desired consistency

**INSTRUCTIONS:**

1. In a blender or food processor, combine cilantro leaves, fresh lime juice, extra-virgin olive oil, and garlic clove.
2. Add honey (or agave syrup if opting for a vegan version), sea salt, and black pepper to the mixture.
3. Process at a high speed until the dressing is smooth and all the components are well incorporated.
4. Gradually add water, one tablespoon at a time, and continue to blend until the dressing reaches your preferred consistency.
5. According to your taste, add more salt, pepper, or lime juice to the dressing to modify the seasoning.
6. The dressing can be used right away or kept for up to a week in the refrigerator in an airtight container.

**Nutritional Information (per serving):** • Calories: 150 kcal • Protein: 0g • Carbohydrates: 8g • Fat: 14g • Saturated Fat: 2g • Cholesterol: 0mg • Sodium: 290mg • Dietary Fiber: 0g • Sugars: 7g

# 18.3 Healthy BBQ Sauce

**Servings: 2 | Preparation Time: 5 minutes | Cook Time: 25 minutes | Total Time: 30 minutes**

## INGREDIENTS:

- 1 can (6 oz / 170g) tomato paste, no salt added
- 1/4 cup (60ml) apple cider vinegar
- 2 tablespoons (30ml) honey or pure maple syrup
- 1 tablespoon Worcestershire sauce (check for a fish-free version if vegetarian)
- 1 teaspoon smoked paprika
- 1/2 teaspoon garlic powder
- 1/2 teaspoon onion powder
- 1/2 teaspoon ground mustard
- 1/4 teaspoon black pepper
- A pinch of cayenne pepper (optional for heat)
- 1 cup (240ml) water, or as needed to adjust consistency

## INSTRUCTIONS:

1. Combine the tomato paste, apple cider vinegar, honey (or maple syrup), and Worcestershire sauce in a medium saucepan over medium heat.
2. Stir in the smoked paprika, garlic powder, onion powder, ground mustard, black pepper, and the optional cayenne pepper for a touch of spiciness.
3. Add water to the mixture, starting with less and adding more as needed to reach your desired sauce consistency.
4. Once all the ingredients are thoroughly mixed, reduce the heat and simmer the mixture.
5. Turn down the heat to low and simmer the sauce for 20-25 minutes, stirring now and again to make sure the flavors combine and to avoid sticking.
6. Once the sauce has thickened to your liking and the flavors have concentrated, remove from heat.
7. Let the sauce cool, then taste and adjust the seasonings if necessary.

**Nutritional Information (per serving, approximately 1/4 cup):**

• Calories: 70 kcal • Protein: 2g • Carbohydrates: 17g • Fat: 0.5g • Saturated Fat: 0g • Cholesterol: 0mg
• Sodium: 90mg • Dietary Fiber: 2g • Sugars: 12g

# 18.4 Lemon Herb Pesto

**Servings: 2 | Preparation Time: 10 minutes | Total Time: 10 minutes**

## INGREDIENTS:

- 1 cup (30g) fresh basil leaves
- 1/2 cup (15g) fresh parsley leaves
- 1/4 cup (30g) raw almonds or pine nuts
- 2 cloves garlic
- Zest of 1 lemon
- 2 tablespoons (30ml) lemon juice
- 1/3 cup (80ml) extra-virgin olive oil
- Salt and pepper, to taste
- Optional: 1/4 cup (25g) grated Parmesan cheese (omit for vegan option)

## INSTRUCTIONS:

1. Put the garlic cloves, almonds (or pine nuts), parsley leaves, and fresh basil leaves in a food processor.

2. Add the ingredients and pulse until roughly chopped.

3. Incorporate the newly squeezed lemon juice and zest into the blend.

4. While the machine is operating, gradually add the extra virgin olive oil until the mixture is thoroughly mixed and the pesto has a creamy, smooth consistency. If required, pause to scrape down the bowl's sides.

5. Season with salt and pepper to taste. If using, stir in the grated Parmesan cheese (or alternative vegan cheese) until well mixed.

6. You may use the pesto right away or keep it in the fridge for up to a week in an airtight container.

**Nutritional Information (per serving):**

• Calories: 390 kcal • Protein: 5g • Carbohydrates: 6g • Fat: 40g • Saturated Fat: 5g • Cholesterol: 4mg
• Sodium: 300mg • Dietary Fiber: 3g • Sugars: 1g

---

# 18.5 Spicy Mustard

**Servings: 2 | Preparation Time: 5 minutes | Resting Time: 4 hours or overnight**
**Total Time: 4 hours 5 minutes**

## INGREDIENTS:

• 1/4 cup (30g) mustard seeds (a mix of yellow and brown for medium heat)
• 2 tablespoons (30ml) apple cider vinegar
• 1/4 cup (60ml) water
• 1 teaspoon (5ml) honey or maple syrup
• 1/2 teaspoon turmeric powder
• 1/4 teaspoon garlic powder
• A pinch of cayenne pepper (adjust to desired heat level)
• Salt to taste

## INSTRUCTIONS:

1. Grind the mustard seeds coarsely in a spice grinder or using a mortar and pestle, leaving some whole for texture.

2. Transfer the ground seeds to a mixing bowl and add apple cider vinegar, water, honey (or maple syrup), turmeric powder, garlic powder, and cayenne pepper.

3. Mix all ingredients thoroughly until well combined.

4. For optimal flavor development, leave the mixture at room temperature for 4 hours or overnight, covered loosely with plastic wrap or a lid.

5. After the resting period, taste the mustard and adjust the flavor with additional honey (for sweetness), vinegar (for tang), or seasonings as desired.

6. Once satisfied with the flavor, the mustard can be used immediately or transferred to an airtight jar and stored in the refrigerator. The flavor will continue to mature over time.

**Nutritional Information (per serving, approximately 2 tablespoons):**

• Calories: 40 kcal • Protein: 2g • Carbohydrates: 4g • Fat: 2g • Saturated Fat: 0g • Cholesterol: 0mg
• Sodium: 80mg • Dietary Fiber: 1g • Sugars: 2g

# CONCLUSION

As we turn the last pages of " The Heart Healthy Cookbook for Beginners," I want to thank you for coming along for the culinary adventure toward a more flavorful and healthier way of living. Eating healthily and heart-healthy doesn't have to mean sacrificing flavor. In fact, it's a chance to experiment with bright flavors and textures and rediscover the joy of cooking excellent meals.

We've included many dishes in this cookbook, from healthy but tempting sweet treats to robust soups, lean proteins, nutrient-dense sides, and vibrant breakfasts and appetizers. Every meal is prepared with your heart health in mind, focusing on whole, wholesome components that enhance general well-being.

Remember that your kitchen is your haven, where you can create, try new things, and enjoy the results of your hard work. This cookbook is meant to empower you, whether a novice or an experienced cook, to make heart-healthy decisions without sacrificing flavor.

I invite you to experiment with, adapt, and customize these dishes to fit your dietary requirements and personal tastes as you continue your culinary travels. There's always space for creativity in the kitchen regarding heart-healthy food, which is a broad field.

May every bite bring you happiness, sustenance, and contentment, and may your heart be as full as your plate. Have fun in the kitchen!

Morgan Alexandra

**"Thank you for dedicating your time to exploring this book.** We genuinely value your thoughts, insights, and feedback. Your unique perspective not only aids fellow readers in determining if this book suits them but also offers invaluable guidance to the author. Every opinion holds significance, and we eagerly anticipate hearing yours."

| amazon.com | amazon.co.uk | amazon.ca |
|:---:|:---:|:---:|
|  |  |  |

# INDEX

Made in the USA
Las Vegas, NV
21 November 2024

12171442R20052